There simply is no magic formula for truly helping people who are materially poor, just as there is no quick solution for those of us who are not! The truth is that we are all deeply broken, and it takes walking together in relationship with God and with one another—over long periods of time—for real change to occur.

Kurt Kandler—co-founder and Executive Director of 410 Bridge—understands this reality. With remarkable candor and endearing humor, Kurt describes his journey from a driven "fixer" of others to the leader of an organization that fosters transformational partnerships between God's people in the U.S. and Majority World. If you really want to help without hurting, Kurt's book is a great place to begin.

—BRIAN FIKKERT
Chalmers Center for Economic Development at Covenant College
Co-author of *When Helping Hurts: How to Alleviate Poverty Without Hurting the Poor . . . and Yourself*

Many traditional Western efforts to do good in the world have resulted in unintended harm. Kurt's work aims to avoid those patterns. The goal: empower communities to create sustained change and create sustained change in those who seek to help. Kurt's leadership has been faithful and consistent, the lessons are clear, their work is proven, and our churches (and many people in them) are better because of our partnership with 410 Bridge.

—ANDY STANLEY
Senior Pastor
North Point Ministries

What is the secret for communities to be lifted out of poverty? It is not what you might think. Kurt Kandler has discovered that secret.

If you have a heart for the poor, be it the poor in your own country or the poor in a distant land, it behooves you to read Kurt's journey in his book, If You Really Want to Help. Kurt found that good intentions do not help the poor and money is not the solution to the problems of poverty. Why? Because lack of money is not the root cause of poverty. If you really want to help the poor, you must go to the root of the problem.

You will find the key to solving the problem of poverty as Kurt shares his own journey of discovery. This key understanding is needed to solve the issue of poverty and will transform people from victimhood to those who are creators of human flourishing.

Read this book!

—Darrow Miller
Author and Cofounder
Disciple Nations Alliance

When my good friend and colleague in development Kurt asked me to consider writing an endorsement for this book, I confess I hesitated. Do we need yet another book on poverty? I wondered. And yet, as I reflected on the reality of many well-meaning development activities in the developing world, I had to admit that an alarming number fail to bring any lasting change. Many well-documented reasons explain this troubling failure. But perhaps the one reason that is least talked about is the failure to transform worldviews and cultural orientations. Kurt believes that mind transformation is an essential catalyst for community transformation. So, yes, we do need another book.

—Sidney Muisyo
Senior Vice President and Chief Program Officer
Compassion International

I've lost track of how many trips I've taken to Kenya since my first trip in 2007. It was then that I met Kurt. It didn't take long to realize that he was someone I wanted to walk and serve with for as long as possible. As the title of the book suggests, he really wants to help. He wants to do all he can with this one life he has been given to love and lead people to become who God wants them to be.

This book lets us know how he's done that for the rural poor in places like Kenya, Haiti, and Guatemala, where dozens of communities have been transformed in recent years. With this book, he invites others to join in that transformation. Readers will find principles and practices that are biblical, logical, and effective. You will also find Kurt to be stubborn enough to keep going despite the challenges, humble enough to admit where he's messed up, and courageous enough to try again and do a little better the next time.

If you just want to feel better about your affluence in a world of poverty, this book isn't for you. If you want an easy solution or a quick fix, this book isn't for you. If you want trite sound bites and snappy slogans, this book isn't for you. But, if you really want to help the billions of poor in our world, if you want to make a lasting impact for the glory of God, if you want to be part of the life-changing movement that the 410 Bridge has begun, Kurt will show you how in this excellent book.

—DR. PAUL McGUINNESS

Director of Intercultural Studies, Clarks Summit University

Author, *Walk This Way*

Kurt's book, If You *Really* Want to Help, *is fast paced and very readable and beautifully captures his journey and transition from the business world to leading 410 Bridge as it follows Christ and impacts the communities where it serves.*

Kurt is transparent about his and his team's failures, is candid with his observations, and doesn't hesitate to call something out when there is need to do so. He vividly captures his reactions to the situations he encounters when he visits the field, to quote, "I'm a high-red, type A, Enneagram 8, ready-fire-aim driver type, always poised for action and never short of an opinion." We need more leaders at the cutting edge like you, Kurt. Leaders like the Apostle Paul, who constantly examined himself and his "assumptions" without hesitating to speak out, or put his hand to the plough, without ever looking back.

The book is powerful and thought provoking. A "must-read" for all leaders who are involved in integral mission and are serious about being Christ followers.

In the ultimate analysis, community participation is not about the community participating in **our programs** *but about us participating in* **their programs**!

—DR. RAVI I. JAYAKARAN

President, Medical Ambassadors International

Catalyst for Integral Mission, the Lausanne Movement

I met Kurt Kandler a little over a year ago. He is a man I immediately loved and respected. We are so much alike in so many ways (age, life experiences, ages of our children, personality, passion, values, etc.). He is my brother and my friend. And my brother and my friend got so much right in his book, If You *Really* Want to Help. *I have traveled to Kenya twice and witnessed some of troubling things he talks about in this book. The difference is that God arrested him in a way that I have never been arrested. Not only did he change his way of life, but he gave him the passion to change the paradigm of how we serve the global poor. His personal story of how God stirred his heart is the proper start for the book. He describes his desire to make a "real" difference in a way that resonates with me and should resonate with you. A "real" difference can be described as positive change that continues from generation to generation. Kurt has done the work. He has made the mistakes. He has created an excellent blueprint. Let's learn from him through this book.*

—ANDRE' KENNEBREW
Director of Relationships
Lifeshape
Prior to Lifeshape spent 15 years at Chick-fil-A

Kurt Kandler has written a must-read for anyone battling the war on poverty. Learn from one of the best leaders working on the front lines and successfully empowering entire communities to lift themselves out of extreme poverty. If you want to make a difference in the lives of those in extreme poverty, read If You *Really* Want to Help *and start your journey to make a difference, the right way.*

—DAN STONAKER
Executive Director, World Missions
North Point Ministries

Do you really want to help the poor? Like, really help them in a way that allows them to be all that God has created them to be? If so, you'll have to let go of some of the ways you've thought, or were taught, were helpful. In the last few decades, governments and NGOs have pumped trillions of dollars in aid into places of poverty like Africa, Haiti, and other majority-world countries. What do we have to show for it besides a refrain of good intentions?

*Kurt's book—*If You *Really* Want to Help*—will prove formative in how the Western church thinks about solving the problem of poverty in a biblical way. When we define poverty as a worldview problem and not simply a material problem, two things happen: we realize our own poverty and that we are not much different from people in the majority world. His book helps all of us properly define the problem and the solution. I'm thankful for Kurt and his boldness to step into this space, providing real solutions that will impact real people in vulnerable communities.*

—JEFF G. FORD
Global Good Pastor
CrossPoint Church—Nashville

IF YOU
REALLY
WANT
TO HELP

IF YOU REALLY WANT TO HELP

REDEFINING THE WAR ON POVERTY

KURT KANDLER

WITH BETHANY BRADSHER

KnE Publishing, LLC • Alpharetta, GA

Published by
KnE Publishing, LLC | Alpharetta, GA

Publisher's Cataloging-in-Publication Data
Kandler, Kurt.

If you really want to help : redefining the war on poverty / Kurt Kandler with Bethany Bradsher. – Alpharetta, GA : KnE Pub., LLC, 2022.

p. ; cm.

ISBN13: 978-0-9601157-0-9

1. Poverty--Uganda. 2. Poor--Uganda. 3. Economic assistance--Uganda. 4. Uganda--Economic conditions--21st century. 5. Uganda--Social conditions--21st century. I. Title. II. Bradsher, Bethany.

HC870.P6 K36 2022
338.91096761--dc23

Project coordination by Jenkins Group, Inc. | www.jenkinsgroupinc.com

Cover design by Jenny Zemanek
Interior design by Brooke Camfield

About the cover photo: Taken in community of Kawira Kenya in 2014, the jump roping girl was captured by Anna Dower. Anna was an intern in Kenya before joining the US staff and ultimately leading our Marketing and Communications team. Anna was struck by the joy, regardless of the circumstances. It reminded her to step outside of herself, her issues and problems and remember what is important about life. Anna is now a successful professional photographer living in Atlanta, Georgia.

Printed in the United States of America
26   25   24   23   22   •   5   4   3   2   1

DEDICATION

I dedicate this book to the love of my life, the amazing Erika. It's been a crazy ride for sure, one filled with unspeakable highs and painfully trying lows. A ride like this would have been impossible without Erika's loving support, encouragement, and grace-filled advice.

And to our newly expanding family . . . Thank you Michael, McKenna, David, and Josh. I was gone more than any of us wanted, but your love and encouragement over the years have been beyond measure. To each of you . . . Go! Be great.

Thank you, Lanny, for your inspiration and for the freedom to lead.

Thanks to all of the 410 Bridge staff over the years, especially those on the front lines. You committed yourselves to helping redefine the war on poverty, what it means to win it, and how we fight the battle together. For that, I am deeply grateful.

Thank you, to the 410 Bridge church partners, donors, and board members. You rode shotgun and faithfully supported the paradigm shift of how we engage the poor.

Thank you, Bethany, for helping me translate the jumbled mess in my head to the written word. You are incredible, and I am grateful for your help.

And, finally, to the leaders and community members I've met and served with over the years. You are the true heroes of the story. You chose to do the hard work. You chose to think differently about the possibilities to live an abundant life. You chose to lead, listen, and run to the mess. You chose to be the solution to the problems around you. Don't stop.

CONTENTS

FOREWORD

Myriad books, TED Talks, and interviews have documented egregious examples of helping that hurts and charity that turns toxic. We are experiencing an awakening to the problems and pitfalls of charity. This awareness is vital. Yet for many, it's also deeply disillusioning—even paralyzing. Afraid of causing harm, some eschew any attempt to help. But *if you really want to help,* averting your eyes and ignoring the reality of pressing needs won't suffice.

I admire Kurt because he is content neither to "help" in a way that's hurting nor to walk away from the needs in our world. Kurt pressed onward past his own initial attempts to effect generational impact in one Ugandan community to discover what truly helps. His book encourages each one of us to do the same. He begins with his personal enthusiasm and excitement about making an impact, and all those who have sought to make a difference in this world will resonate with his enthusiasm, idealism, drive, and perhaps unintended hubris as he set out to change a community 8,000 miles from home. But bringing his heart and head, as well as a willingness to listen, over time, Kurt "failed forward" into a different model. He shares candidly the lessons he's learned the hard way but goes on to highlight hope-filled stories of success.

Kurt committed to the hard work of looking failure in the face and determining how to really help. He doesn't stop with telling us what *not to do*; he points to what we should do *if we really want to help.* Instead of highlighting the flaws in others' approach or criticizing from the sidelines, Kurt vulnerably relates his own "mortifying" early attempts. But Kurt humbly acknowledged and identified the shortcomings of his approach and was willing to change. He recognized how much he didn't know, then listened, learned, and improved.

If You Really *Want to Help* is a book for those eager to move beyond good intentions. It's a blueprint for how to think about our long-term impact on communities around the world. It highlights the holistic approach pioneered by Kurt and his team at 410 Bridge, where they help communities define and achieve success across the areas of water, economic development, health, education, and discipleship.

Kurt may have charged headlong into a Ugandan community in 2005, but today 410 Bridge waits to be invited. They serve alongside, not in the place of, community members and local churches. They never presume that their help is wanted, and they elevate internal solutions rather than imposing external ones.

I have seen this approach firsthand as I've traveled with Kurt to see the work of 410 Bridge in Haiti. At HOPE International, we partner with 410 Bridge in additional countries because we deeply respect not only what they do but also how they do it. I admire their holistic focus and their strategy to go deep rather than wide in community development. They are committed to true transformation within the communities they serve, and it all began with a work of transformation in Kurt's own life when he courageously adopted a new approach.

Kurt committed to relationships rather than projects and sustained transformation rather than charity. He reimagined the traditional roles of giver and receiver to create relationships of reciprocity and respect. He committed to asking better questions and to truly listening to those who responded. Kurt is a challenger, who began with a willingness to challenge his own assumptions. This book will challenge yours as well. *If You* Really *Want to Help* not only begins with the story of a transformational journey but also initiates one. The book invites you to see differently, think differently, and respond differently, if you *really* want to help.

Peter Greer
President & CEO of HOPE International
Author, *The Spiritual Danger of Doing Good*

CHAPTER ONE

It was hard to believe, but there we were—Entebbe International Airport. I had worked toward this moment for a long time. Some might say I had "dreamed" of this moment for a long time, but that's not accurate. It wasn't that aspirational. The truth was I just wanted to help.

I had learned about a need, worked hard to raise the money, planned as much as I could, and muscled through the long, cramped flight. As we gathered our children and all of our carry-ons to deplane, I looked to my wife and three young children, smiled nervously, and said, "Well? Here we are!" It was going to be an exciting adventure.

Whatever sense of accomplishment I may have felt was quickly replaced with doubts as soon as we joined the long immigration line. I hadn't been off the plane for five minutes and I was already questioning this decision. Guards in camo fatigues with automatic rifles were posted every several feet. They looked suspiciously at everyone. The cold, hard feel of the bright fluorescent lights was dimmed only slightly by the thousands of flying insects they attracted. The 1970s-era construction added to the realization that I had just stepped into an environment I knew nothing about.

We were hypersensitive to the bugs. Weird, I know. But in order to get any level of buy-in from our parents to take their grandchildren to Uganda, we had to promise to get jabbed with every inoculation recommended. We had taken so many shots and pills that I was sure we glowed. Yellow fever, malaria, typhoid, tetanus, hepatitis, you name it . . . It didn't stand a chance in the Kandler family. But the negotiation with our parents made us all the more nervous about getting sick, so our perception was that "it" (whatever "it" might be) was everywhere. And most of "it" was courtesy of these little flying menaces. Some were small, but others not so much. A few of them hovered over us every few minutes, and we felt the breeze of their wings.

Naturally, both sets of our parents had tried to talk us out of all this, but my response went something like, "I got this. It's going to be fine. What could go wrong?" But now, in the moments immediately after leaving the safety of our KLM 747-400 and perhaps a little too late, I wondered whether I should have lingered over that question a little longer. After all, lots could actually go wrong. And what had I done to *really* prepare? What did I *really* know about any of this?

The murderous LRA (Lord's Resistance Army), led by the Ugandan warlord and lunatic Joseph Kony, was in the news at the time for abducting children and turning them into child soldiers. My generation—and my parents'—hadn't shaken the memory of Idi Amin, a ruthless dictator who had killed up to half a million of his people during his reign in the '70s. And then there was AIDS, which had decimated families by the early 2000s, lowering the average age in Uganda to fifteen years old. All of this occupied my mind as my family slowly inched our way through the line, ducking every so often to miss the swooping bugs, until the immigration officer stamped our passports and welcomed us to Uganda.

WARNING—SHARP TURN AHEAD

If you had told me eighteen months earlier that in 2005 I would be leading my family to East Africa to build a school, I would have laughed. We lived in a safe, comfortable Atlanta suburb. I loved it there, and to this point in my life I hadn't thought one iota about the issues facing the developing world. But life can throw surprising curveballs.

I had built a career as an entrepreneur, and by then I was dealing with the remains of a post-9/11 failed business. Like many business owners at that time, I found that the effects of 9/11 were too much for my marketing agency to withstand. When I finally pulled the plug in 2003, the fallout of some bad decisions and a mountain of personally guaranteed debt consumed my every thought. Erika's anxiety about the growing debt, the mounting bills, and my need to make wiser decisions weighed heavily on me. Understandably, my worry over the present didn't allow any room for thoughts of people struggling with extreme poverty, until my friend Dave showed me some photos and I found myself, improbably, on a path even I didn't understand.

We knew Dave and his family from our children's elementary school in Atlanta. As part of their Christmas generosity drive, the students filled shoeboxes of supplies they thought Ugandan students would like, and in 2004, Dave took his family of six and all of the shoeboxes to a sister school of about ninety students in Butalale (BOO-ta-LA-lee), Uganda. When he returned, we hosted a group at our home for coffee and dessert so he could share some photos and stories from his trip.

I respected Dave. He was a straight shooter and not a man prone to exaggeration or superlatives. When he shared his family's experience, it was believable and understated. It seemed to me that the people he visited over there lacked, well . . . *every*thing. No water. No electricity. No indoor plumbing. No income opportunities. No health facilities. The school (if you could call it that) had a few desks and no textbooks, paper, or writing materials. The school building itself is what captured my attention: dirt floors, a rusted and leaky metal roof, and walls made of mud, sticks, and cow dung. Every time a rainstorm blew through, the parents had to repack and reform the walls. The classroom was dirty, dark, and hot. The students who arrived early were rewarded by being crammed five or six together on rickety bench seats. For the not so fortunate, a small rock was their seat for the day. There were no trained teachers, no textbooks, no school supplies—not even chalk for the painted blackboard on the mud wall.

As Dave worked through his photos, I was present, listening, but not *really* there. I was distracted—distracted by my perception of myself as an outsider looking in on this successful group of families. The other couples knew of our troubles. We would soon have to withdraw our children from the school for financial reasons, and I was certain that everyone around me could see that our family was no longer part of the same circle. I saw myself as a *failed* business guy. I was sure that others perceived me the same way. I had always told myself that failure was inevitable and acceptable as long as I "failed forward," but during that season, I had failed, and it sure didn't feel forward. I would have been fine with just being stuck. But I wasn't stuck; I was sliding backward quickly. I refer to this season as our "dark times." I knew that others had faced darker circumstances than us—loss of a loved one, health crises, addiction—but for me, this was the lowest point in my forty-plus-year life. It was hard to imagine ever returning to a place of flourishing.

The fear, uncertainty, broken trust, and insecurities that marked that period affected every choice I made. I had failed, and I had to fix it. But to fix it, I had to find solutions, and I didn't have any. My situation was all I could think about, until Dave showed us the photo of a dilapidated village school building. That's when I started to dial in to a different problem.

My reaction to those pictures was pretty typical of my personality. I'm a high-red, type A, Enneagram 8, ready-fire-*aim* driver type, always poised for action and never short of an opinion. I've never been much for protracted planning; if I see something that needs to be done, I'm already taking the first steps toward doing it. See a problem, solve a problem. I had some construction experience in my first business, and the sad state of that school building seemed, well . . . a little baffling. "That seems kinda silly," I said to Dave. "Why don't they just build a brick building? It's not *that* hard to do." Dave's response was simple: "I don't know."

The next morning, I was in my basement office, working furiously to serve the few clients I had left from my business. It wasn't going well. I was fearful and anxious. But despite the obvious need to focus on my work, the Butalale school kept pushing its way back into my mind. I felt drawn to it, but I knew it wasn't the time to exert brain sweat on that school. My family needed me, depended on me. I should be focused on rebuilding my career, not rebuilding an African school. But the image of that cow dung building kept capturing my thoughts.

So I let myself focus on it, and soon I was brokering a not-so-uncommon negotiation with my Creator that went something like this: "Tell ya what I'm gonna do . . ." (He loves it when we negotiate!) "When I get my business back on track and start making some money again . . . when I get my kids back into private school and get all of this debt paid off . . . when I right this ship . . . I'll go over there and build those Butalale kids a brick building! Deal?" But before I could even finish my offer, it was made clear to me that I had it backward. As foolhardy as it seemed, I needed to build those kids that building. As for the crisis that still raged all around me, well, that would have to be dealt with too. But it was clear: that building was important. I wanted to help. I was supposed to help.

And then the realization hit me: the fear of what came next. You know, the dread that sounds a lot like "Yeesh," followed by the churning of the stomach. It wasn't the money. I didn't know how, but I'd find the money. It wasn't the logistics. I could muscle through all of those. The daunting first step was . . . Erika.

My wife of now thirty-one-plus years is nothing less than amazing. Actually, the word "amazing" seems inadequate. Add a few more superlatives to that and you'll come to better understand my deep love, admiration, and respect for her. At this time, understandably, Erika needed stability—both for our children and from a husband who needed to be focused on a financial dumpster fire. This school building idea, by any reasonable standard, would be distracting and unnecessary. I knew she couldn't even begin to share my conviction for it, because she was so focused on our day-to-day survival. This made for a fascinating conversation starter that day.

But something was working in Erika too. Neither of us knew it or saw it, but it was there. To label her skeptical would be a massive understatement, but she loved me, and if I felt led to help, she said I should try. So somehow, miraculously, beyond reason, she agreed to join me in trying to build a school in a place we had never visited that was almost eight thousand miles away.

I continued to wrestle with the idea, talking to Dave about all the complexities of actually doing such a thing. It became clear that the first step was to raise money, and with Dave's help I contacted Peterson, his contact in Uganda, and learned that the school building would cost $10,000. But that was only a fraction of the actual price tag. As it turned out, it was more than just a school building. The school needed water, electricity, and road-work to even get the materials to the school. All of it was over $40,000! I started asking friends for donations, and they began to trickle in, but it was slow going. It took eighteen months just to raise the $10,000 for the school.

Raising $40,000 seemed completely unattainable, so after we had enough for the building, I decided to pull the trigger on the trip. I was concerned that my network had grown weary of hearing me dwell on needing money for an obscure project halfway around the world. But once we announced that the trip was a reality, it sparked more donations. I guess it became real for my friends too. By the time we left the day after Christmas in 2005, I felt like we had the resources we needed to make a *real* difference in Butalale. My buddy Dave agreed to go with us, so we set about making our travel plans, scheduling inoculations, and figuring out how to pack for a family of five on a multiweek trip to Africa.

WELCOME TO BUTALALE

And that's the quick version of the winding path that led us to a bug-infested airport and, before we could even catch our breath, on a harrowing trip to congested Kampala and then across bumpy dirt roads to the rural community of Butalale. During our first few days, I couldn't shed the trepidation that I was putting my family at risk, and alongside that anxiety was a barrage of new sights, sounds, and experiences. You can read books, see photos, and watch videos, but books and pictures don't really prepare you for the experience of rural East Africa. I tell people that they have to "smell it." That doesn't mean that it smells; it just means that until you are immersed in it, you can't connect with it.

Herds of livestock travel along the side of the roads, even congested city roadways. People are everywhere—walking, sitting, selling wares in open markets. Women and young children haul heavy water containers on their backs in the morning, then repeat the same routine in the afternoon, only the water is replaced with a heavy load of firewood. Motorcycles and bicycles fill the streets carrying all manner of things—people, water, animals, and building materials. It wasn't uncommon to see a motorcycle transporting a couch, a table, a chest of drawers! The layers of fine dirt that settle into everything. The lack of infrastructure. The dirt roads with potholes large enough to swallow a hatchback.

Despite the sensory overload, my prevailing mood as I undertook the new school construction was hope. Don't misunderstand. I'm generally not a big fan of the word "hope," because

The Butalale school upon our arrival.

I subscribe to the "hope is not a strategy" mindset. I value action and planning over some obscure and immeasurable feeling of expectation. But now I found myself in an environment that was impossible to control. I wanted this to work. This needed to work. I had talked this up to everyone who would listen for nearly two years, and I *hoped* it would be worth the time and money that had been provided. I *hoped* my family would be safe, and I looked forward to the prospect of seeing the completed school. I was over there to solve a problem, and I *hoped* to leave with the feeling of satisfaction that comes when a project is completed. I *hoped* people's lives would improve because of it. After all, I had *really* good intentions, and I just wanted to help.

We arrived in the rural village of Butalale. It isn't really a village in the sense that we would think of a village. It's more of a grassy plain with dozens of footpaths leading to small multi-structure compounds. Every so often you could see one of the homesites through the tall grass. As we navigated the bumpy road (more of a path) and arrived at the work site in Butalale for the first time, I saw that, as we had planned, hired workers had already laid the foundation and erected the four corner pillars for the new building's walls. We had sent money ahead for those preliminary tasks so that we could jump right in once we arrived. And jump right in was exactly what I was anxious to do, but first a crowd of women and children greeted us with song and dance. They were warm and hospitable. Huge, cheerful smiles. Incredibly joyful. It would be that joy that would have an effect on me and my family forever. Everyone introduced themselves, and we were eager to capture all of the festivities digitally.

The Kandler boys laying bricks.

We were deeply encouraged by their welcome, even though I felt awkward about all the attention and I was ready to get to work. But something unsettled me on that first day in the village. Despite the hospitality from the women and children, I was struck by the fact that the local men were nowhere to be found. It was literally all women and children. The only men were the paid laborers working on the school. I put that thought behind me, and we spent that afternoon meeting the people who had gathered and getting acquainted with the village. We would start construction the next morning.

On our first full workday, we learned about the multiweek process the locals use to make homemade mud bricks—forming them from mud, stacking them into a homemade kiln, and firing them for several days. We purchased prepared bricks from local producers, and we layered each one with cement to assemble the school walls. At first, all six of us were "helping," even though I had a strong hunch we were slowing the hired workers down. It was hot, dirty, grueling work, and I wasn't too surprised when Erika and the kids quickly moved to other things. The Butalale women invited Erika and our daughter McKenna to their homes scattered throughout the village.

We settled into a daily rhythm: Dave and I and my two young sons, Michael and David, would spend the days at the worksite. By midmorning the boys would get pulled away by the local children and spend the rest of the day playing nearby. There wasn't really anything to play *with*, so they played with *anything*. The boys would find long sticks and try to "pole-vault" over small ditches. They'd make a ball out of plastic bags and string and play soccer or dodgeball. We were repeatedly struck by the people. We had come with a view that they were suffering in poverty. And, yes, in a sense they were. But they were also full of dignity and hospitality, not casualties of their circumstances. They were determined to be the perfect hosts, to make our children feel welcome and entertained. Even with just sticks and plastic bags, they found a way to make the day fun.

And, then, another reality check. As the sun and heat made our children thirsty, they went to the van for bottled water, a luxury not available to the local children. The nearest water source was about a mile away from the village. We hadn't brought enough water for the entire community, and it was a harsh reminder of their daily reality. When we disposed of an empty water bottle, every single one was retrieved by our hosts. I wondered whether our children would be as joyful, inviting, and generous with so little. It was a thought that captured me, and I knew the answer. Erika and the kids spent a good deal of time in the village getting to know the women and their families—visiting home after home, learning the ways of the locals.

We were exhausted by bedtime, but Erika and I tried to debrief every night to process our distinct experiences. Even though we intended this to be a family adventure, the truth was that we hardly saw each other during the day. I was head-down laboring on the school building, concerned about whether we would complete the project in time. I had little time for anything else. Erika would remind me daily that I needed to join her in meeting the families. But the way I saw it, I had a job to do, and that didn't allow for the "luxury" of slowing down and having conversations.

Erika was full of stories about Butalale hospitality, the people she was meeting, and her up-close look at the extreme poverty she had never witnessed before. She visited one home, probably ten to fifteen feet square, that had five people living on one side of the dividing wall and the family's cow and calf living on the other. The cows were so important to their financial well-being that they needed to spend precious space in their tiny house to keep them safe. Erika was being stretched in all kinds of ways but never as much as when several of the local mothers told her that they didn't have enough money for their children's school fees. After several appeals, she decided that since it wasn't much and she had the money, she would help a couple of her new friends. It was a well-intended decision with toxic repercussions.

She gave some money to one woman and told another she would give her some the next day, but when other ladies from the village warned her that the second woman would spend it on alcohol, Erika didn't know what to do. And, of course, it didn't stop. The same group of women would follow her everywhere, every day. Most of the community had been so kind to her, opening their homes, explaining how they lived, talking about their lives, but Erika knew she had created a disruption. So many people needed help just as much as the women who had asked for the school fees. Erika could tell from the looks of the woman she didn't help, and the comments from those who hadn't asked for anything, that her generosity was causing division and jealousy among neighbors—fallout she certainly never intended.

At night, when we talked over the things we had seen and experienced each day, it became clear to me that this impulse to go overseas and help—to do a good thing—was far more complicated than it had seemed from our home in the comfortable suburbs of Atlanta. I still felt like we were meant to do this, but as the week went on, I wondered whether our extended families were right and I was, in fact, crazy to attempt it.

Although most of my focus was on getting the school walls constructed, during one of our days in Butalale we undertook a family project that we had planned while we were still in the States. Each of us had packed an extra army duffel bag of clothes, shoes, and other supplies with the intention of giving those away to the "poor Ugandans." We also went on a shopping spree in Kampala (the capital) to buy books and other supplies for the school. Once we had all of the wares we wanted to give away, we set up a table under a large tent, organized the clothes and shoes by sizes, and invited each person in the large gathering crowd to partake in our generosity.

After ten days in Butalale, it was time to leave and return to the world we knew. As we were about to depart, to our amazement, the community gathered to give us a proper farewell. One by one they came to give us a small token of their appreciation—a handmade rug, a bracelet, a necklace. In one example of sacrificial generosity, a young woman was so thankful for our visit that she gave Erika her only chicken, the value of which was not lost on us.

We had finished the school building right on time, save the metal roof, which the workers would install after we left. We had given clothes and books to people in need. Our entire family had immersed ourselves in another culture for a couple weeks, and if we were to host our own dessert and coffee to share photos and stories, anyone in attendance would surely conclude that we had done something significant.

But I knew better.

Just two or three days into the trip, I was disillusioned with the whole thing. For much of the trip, I was so unsettled I could hardly sleep. And when I look back on it today, I'm mortified by some of the things we did.

The Kandler family nearing the end of the visit to Butalale.

TROUBLING REALIZATIONS

I remember talking to Erika one night in our stark hotel room after the kids had gone to sleep. "The issues here are way bigger than this school building," I told her. "I guess we're helping with this school and the water project, but it is of no moment. It doesn't matter. What we're doing is a tiny drop in a really big bucket."

I had expected that our efforts would make a *real* difference—a difference for generations. Generations of kids would attend school in the new building. Generations of families would partake of safe water. But as I've heard so often, "Disappointment comes from unmet expectations." And was I ever disappointed.

Questions begat more questions. Where were the men in Butalale? I hardly saw any, and those I did see had no interest in helping with the school. Where was the community ownership of the needs or the plans to address the needs that we couldn't? Why were there so many unfinished buildings everywhere? How did people live without access to safe water? Why did all of the nicest vehicles seem to have logos of the UN or other aid organizations? Why did the actions we thought would be beneficial for people actually have the opposite effect?

To be clear, Erika was incredible. She tried to reassure me, but deep down she saw what I saw—an overwhelming patchwork of desperate needs and unfinished projects that appeared nothing more than monuments to the well-intentioned Westerners who came, did, and moved on to other things that interested them. Driving to and from Butalale each day, we saw dozens and dozens of "projects" incomplete or in very poor condition. So many had come before us with the same desire to help—to fix a problem—but hadn't succeeded. I saw the issues more clearly, to be sure, but what I didn't see at that stage was a clear path to solutions.

Since Erika and I are wired very differently, our experiences in Butalale represent two typical and distinct ways Westerners react when they serve people struggling with poverty. There are people like me: all action, results oriented, tackling every problem they see with a budget and a three-step plan whether the "beneficiaries" are asking for our version of intervention or not. We may candy coat and justify it, but in the end, it's our money and our idea, so it's our way.

Then there are those who are more like Erika: big heart, kind, and conflict averse. So anxious to smooth over the hardships

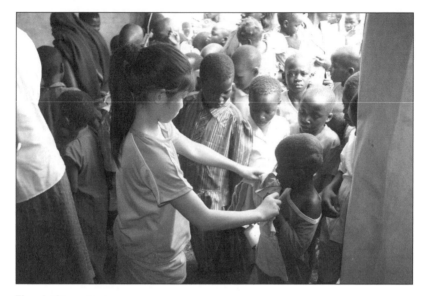

The clothing giveaway.

they see that their actions, like giving money for school fees, stir up more problems than they solve.

And that family project we did—the big clothing giveaway—was one of the most problematic. We both saw it even as it was unfolding before us. "It was complete chaos," Erika recalled. "Everybody was grabbing for things, and the people who were polite and waited at the end of the line like they were supposed to had nothing left when they finally came to the front. It came from good intentions, but it was a bad idea. People didn't get the things that they wanted or needed. It encouraged poor behavior. It encouraged jealousy, and it stripped the women of their dignity."

Near the end of our time in Butalale I had a few minutes to sit down with Peterson, who had organized our visit. Full of plans for a campus, he grabbed a stick and started to draw the school property in the dust on the new floor of the building. He drew a small rectangle signifying the building we had just finished and then told me about his vision for dormitories, more classroom blocks, administration buildings, latrines, and a variety of other improvements for the school. I smiled and confessed, "Look, man . . . It took me almost two years just to do this project, and my network is tapped out." I was grateful for Peterson's vision, but the whole exchange left me feeling defeated. I was disillusioned, but underneath that dark cloud was my strong hunch that there actually was, in fact, a way to move the proverbial needle. I wasn't sure what it was, but I was certain what it wasn't. It wasn't what we had just done or how we had done it.

A MYTH BUSTED

When we left Uganda, I didn't feel that the trip was a mistake; in fact, I was sure it was something I was meant to do. But the uneasiness that had started a few days after our arrival revealed a deep disconnect between our activity and our accomplishment. This whole thing started because I just wanted to help. Sure . . . we helped, but had we *really* helped? Simply wanting to help wasn't enough. My good intentions weren't good enough, and the chasm between just wanting to help and *really* helping revealed a myth that *anything* we do for the poor must be a good thing. It's not.

The only thing I knew for sure was that I wasn't sure what to do. But as anyone who knows me will tell you, in times of confusion, conflict, and uncertainty, I'm just going to do the next right thing.

CHAPTER TWO

I am asked quite often, especially from "halftime" men who may be struggling with the tension between seeking success and seeking significance, how it was that I would leave the private sector during the season of my life that would arguably be my greatest income-producing years to start a small nonprofit focused on the global poor. There are many people who feel the same internal passions that I was struggling with in early 2006. They see a need and want to help. Something may be stirring in their soul—a desire to do something bigger, better, or more meaningful than their current pursuits.

Identifying that stirring is difficult and very personal. To leave the comfort and security of what we know for the risk and uncertainty of what we don't can be paralyzing. I was caught in a tug-of-war between the pursuit of professional and financial stability and this crazy idea that had lodged itself in my brain—that there had to be a better way to *really* help the poor, an approach that would *really* lift them out of extreme poverty and not just address symptoms.

There's a progression that we all go through at times like this, and my journey was no different. It starts with the notion of what *could* be done. An idea is formed. It's possible. It was on my mind to do, but more theoretical than anything else. There was plenty I didn't understand, but I was confident that this was a problem that *could* be solved, even if that *could* tilted more toward the theoretical than the actionable.

From *could,* I moved to *should.* This *should* be done and goes beyond possibility to a sort of moral imperative. I wrestled with my conviction that helping the poor was important. It demanded my attention. It was the right thing to do, and there was a lot at stake if it didn't happen. It was something that *should* be done. I believed that strongly.

But while *could* and *should* are vital steps, nothing is ever going to happen until what *could* be done, and what *should* be done, moves to what *must* be done. That radical step to leave the marketplace and leap into the unknown would never have happened without the *must.* Moving from "I could . . ." to "I should . . ." was easy. After all, I saw myself as capable, teachable, and willing to leverage my skills and experience for the cause. But when I jumped to "I *must* do this," it became an issue of identity. I couldn't deny that what I had done to this point wasn't really all that helpful. I couldn't look the other way or continue to ignore what I saw and experienced. And, importantly, I couldn't put on blinders or simply ignore the lack of true impact and transformation that came from my time in Butalale just for the sake of feeling good about helping.

That wasn't going to cut it. I had changed, and going back to what I knew before simply wasn't possible.

It was time to step through the door. I didn't really have a choice. I couldn't go back to the person I was. Weird, but that's why it turns into an identity issue. When we *must* do something, it changes us. It changes who we are and what we prioritize, and it reveals to us that even more change is needed. And therein lay one of my biggest challenges. I *really* wanted to help. I wanted to *truly* make a difference in the lives of people living in extreme poverty so that they never would again. But in order to do that, I needed to change my way of thinking. To what? From what? Part of the problem was the way I thought about poverty, the poor, and the methods to help.

Clearly, what I had originally thought was going to make a generational impact in Butalale would not. It wasn't that the kids in Butalale didn't need a permanent school building. They did, and I'm happy that they got one. It wasn't that the school didn't need access to safe water or textbooks. It did, and I'm sure they're grateful. But solving the school building problem and the water problem wasn't going to solve the *poverty* problem. In order for that to happen, I needed to change my way of thinking about both the problem and the solutions.

WANTED: A PLAN

The focus of my attention was moving from the school in Butalale to the broader issues that kept the Butalale people living in extreme poverty. I knew that simply helping with the school addressed a small part of a broader problem. The lack of infrastructure was obvious—not just the lack of a school, but roads, power, water, health care, marketplaces . . . everything. And then there was the undeniable reality that, in the future, any well-meaning actions could harm the very people we were looking to help. I kept thinking back to that clothing distribution in Butalale. All those free clothes, and the battles they sparked, not only caused tension but also might very well have put any small business that did sell clothes out of business and caused more hardship not just for the small store owner but also for the people in the village.

But another undeniable lesson from Butalale became clear to me as I reflected on my days building the school. The people there had skills; they made the bricks and laid them much better than I ever could. They were capable, and once the building was complete, they were justifiably proud of their new school. Any solution had to include respecting their culture, which meant recognizing their skills and gifts. As I looked toward a new year, my mind churned, and I felt compelled to investigate options.

There were two burning questions. My Butalale trip had started to cement my understanding of what *not* to do, but, first, how could I define what *to* do and make that plan a reality? And, second, where would the money come from to support the work?

A NEW COLLABORATION

My trip to Uganda had left me with one thread I could follow when I returned to Atlanta. A few years earlier, Peterson had attended a conference in my home city. At that conference, he met a man named Lanny Donoho, and Peterson mentioned Lanny as someone I should get to know. When he mentioned Lanny's name to me, I knew who he was immediately. I didn't know Lanny personally, but I knew *of* Lanny. He was one of the leaders in the children's program at our church, North Point Community Church. He was a bit of a celebrity in our church, bringing a crazy and comedic element to Sunday mornings. He was also the founder and director of BigStuf Camp, a huge summer youth camp in Panama City Beach. Lanny had no idea who I was, but I had a hunch that if he shared my interest in engaging with the poor in a new way, he could help me connect with the leaders of North Point and potentially lots of other people with similar interests.

Lanny graciously agreed to meet Erika and me for dinner in early 2006. The conversation became promising as he sketched the early lines of a vision that intersected with the stirrings I had been feeling. He had been taking some college interns to Kenya, and he was really struck by the transformation he saw in the young people who went. Lanny shared that he was thinking about doing something in East Africa, but he didn't want to do what everybody else was doing. Lanny would say, and I would completely agree, that he thinks differently from most people. If it's been done, it doesn't hold his attention.

We agreed that traditional methods weren't working and that it was time to try something new, something that could really change lives. I think we were both frustrated by the fact that after so much time and money, rural East Africa, like many sub-Saharan African countries, hadn't kept pace with the development across the globe that has moved people out of absolute poverty. Food insecurity, poor infrastructure, primitive living, and lack of clean water and access to energy have kept communities there stuck in place. Governments and NGOs had come to help, but it wasn't moving the needle.

Lanny and I were coming at it from different perspectives— Lanny from the point of view of the people who went overseas and me from the point of view of the people living in poverty— but we were both set on disrupting the spaces where things had been done the same way for years and years.

What Lanny said next at dinner resonated with me. "I stand up in front of tens of thousands of people each year, hundreds and hundreds of churches and organizations. What if . . . ?" he asked. "What if we got all those people and all those organizations to focus on one place? Do you think we could move the needle in that place? Do you think we could move the needle in that place to such a degree that the places around that place saw the difference and asked, 'Why is it different over there? Why are the children healthier and better educated? Why do they have clean water? Why do they have more economic opportunity?' What if the answers to those questions pointed back to a small, disruptive organization in Atlanta that decided to do this whole thing differently?"

I left that meeting more than slightly intrigued. I was becoming more and more convinced that I had an idea of how to execute on Lanny's "move the needle" vision. It would take a deeper understanding of the problems, of course, but it would also take unyielding focus and discipline to execute well. Over time,

I worked my way from "I *could* do this" to "I *should* do this" to "I *must* do this."

This prompted another memorable conversation with my better half. Admittedly, Erika wasn't convinced real change could happen. To her the problems seemed insurmountable. But she believed in me, and she believed that if I had a vision for that kind of change, I should move forward with her full support.

CREATIVITY MEETS DISCIPLINE

Lanny is an uber-creative visionary, and that's actually an understatement. He dreams, casts vision, and approaches problems from a completely different perspective than I do. Lanny acknowledges, however, that he needs other people to help him make those dreams a reality. While they're off doing that, he's often onto the next big idea. I had come to understand this about him, and I felt like he would receive and understand what I wanted to propose.

At our next meeting, I got right to the point: "When we met for dinner, you shared your idea of mobilizing tens of thousands of people and hundreds of churches to move the needle in one place. I was captured by that idea, but, with all due respect, you don't strike me as the kind of guy who can pull that off." If Lanny hadn't already detected my propensity for bluntness, he did at that moment. He wasn't offended. He chuckled and said, "You're probably right."

Unlike Lanny, who was pulled in multiple directions, I was focused on the solutions and execution for the problem I had started to understand in Butalale. Ideas had begun to form in my mind. To me it was clear that there were a lot of Americans who saw the suffering of the poor and wanted to help, but their efforts were driven by emotion or pet projects. The result was temporary help that often came with a dose of harm. I wasn't all that emotional about it. I was matter-of-fact as I told Lanny that I thought I knew how to go about sparking significant and permanent change in poor communities. I thought I had an idea for moving the needle on the other side of the bridge, but I knew that I needed Lanny's help to rally support stateside.

Lanny's reputation as a guy who had exciting ideas and could make big things happen had preceded him, and when word started to spread that he was considering an initiative in Kenya, people came out of the woodwork wanting to be a part of it. To keep their attention, Lanny asked those people to research specific problems that existed in poor communities in East Africa. He created need-oriented groups in areas like safe water, orphan care, education, economic development, food insecurity, HIV/AIDS, and others.

In all, ten "task forces" were created. They gathered data and research results and crafted possible interventions to address their specific problem topic. When they had compiled their findings, Lanny asked me to attend a meeting to listen to their presentations. Each person who spoke that day was passionate about the area they represented. They were excited to help. From what I could see, they did a good job, but nothing was said about the ways in which the various needs intersected or the importance of approaching development holistically.

Before the presentations were over, Lanny had to leave for another appointment (a real bummer for those who hadn't shared their findings yet) and I followed him out of the room. That session had only heightened my conviction that development work would never be impactful if it bounced from one "passion project" to another. I felt certain that we needed a systematic, focused, and disciplined plan that would lead to self-sustaining solutions. We needed to go a mile deep in a community with a goal of sustainable change. The task forces saw poverty as a set of problems to be solved. Their approaches were an inch deep and a mile wide.

As Lanny and I talked outside that meeting room, he saw that my enthusiasm hadn't waned. I appreciated that he got right to the point. He asked me why a forty-something father of three, with lots of needs and attachments, should lead a new international nonprofit. Why not find someone in their twenties or thirties who would be freer to travel and less concerned about financial obligations? It was a valid point, but I thought he was asking the wrong question.

I told him: "This effort, if we do it right, is going to require focus and strong, disciplined leadership. This is an incredibly emotional space, especially when it comes to children. You can't swing a dead cat without hitting a need over there, and strong leadership isn't required to determine what we *are* going to do; strong leadership is required to determine what we're *not* going to do."

I pointed back to the room we just left. "You have a dozen-plus people in there representing different passions. And each of their passions is their top priority. In my view, 70 percent of them need to be told that their ideas and solutions, while arguably helpful, aren't going to happen. We'll never have enough time, talents, or resources to do *everything*, and our ability to stay focused and disciplined on what actually moves the needle is going to require strong leadership. I have the temperament and discipline to determine not just what *to* do but what *not* to do." As years at 410 would later prove, it is extremely difficult to say no. When we say no, people suffer. But saying no—resisting being blown by the emotional winds—has proven crucial to being effective.

That may have been the closing argument that brought Lanny and me together, prompting a decision that neither of us ever regretted. Lanny chose to trust me with my vision for the development plan, while I trusted him with his vision on this side of the bridge. One of my first concrete steps in constructing this new entity was a trip to Florida to see BigStuf in action.

A BRIDGE TAKES SHAPE

The idea for a new organization was closer to reality, but not real yet, when I visited BigStuf that summer. I had never experienced anything like it, and I saw the potential for our fledgling effort to get in front of a significant number of people from the platform Lanny had created. While 410 Bridge would ultimately help hundreds of thousands of people in the countries where we work, we knew that the bridge was two way. It's been humbling to hear stories about how it has affected people at home. Dozens of the churches attending BigStuf were willing to try new methods and would eventually have successful partnerships with 410.

Hundreds of students from BigStuf would go on to life-changing experiences with 410.

Later that summer Lanny approached a generous donor about the new venture, explained the vision, and came away with a commitment to provide enough funding for one year. In the nine months since my family had battled bugs and disenchantment in Butalale, a passion had formed, a chance introduction from a Ugandan pastor to Lanny had happened, and all the start-up funds were in place. And just like that, I became the cofounder and executive director of 410 Bridge. We started with a staff of one . . .

WHERE TO GO, WHAT TO DO

We launched 410 Bridge on September 1, 2006. We chose to start in Kenya because we had more relationships and connections with other organizations in Kenya than in Uganda. I would leave for Kenya in October of that year to lay some groundwork. I would visit Kenya more than fifty times over the next fifteen years, but this first trip would be dedicated to meeting local leaders who had connections to people I knew in the US. I needed to find a few communities that might be candidates for partnership—places where we could establish relationships and start laying the groundwork to drive change.

Before our official start, Lanny and BigStuf had embarked on a short list of small projects, including renovations to a pastor's home in a rural community called Kwambekenya. Boniface, who lived in the house, was a young pastor just getting started in Kwambekenya, a unique community located about three hours north of Nairobi. Unlike many of the agrarian communities in East Africa where family land is passed down through generations, Kwambekenya didn't exist at all until 1988. That was the year the Kenyan government forced hundreds of families out of the forest where they made their living "illegally" harvesting the forest trees. Since the people were forced to evacuate their land, and with no place to go, the Mbekenya family made about 100 acres of its farmland available for purchase. Community members purchased small plots (a quarter to a half acre) and settled. That's how Kwambekenya gets its name: "Kwa," meaning "belonging to" Mbekenya.

Remember those task forces I spoke of earlier? I connected with Boniface through the guy who spearheaded the research on education, Steve Smith, who was going to visit Kenya with another organization a few weeks before my scheduled trip in October. He joined a medical team visiting a children's home in Central Kenya. I met Steve for the first time at that task force presentation. He, too, was a business guy, and we became quick friends. Years later Steve would become our COO, but during this trip he agreed to be on the lookout for communities that I might be interested in meeting during my first visit.

Steve's days in-country were filled by working alongside a small group of local and American medical professionals in multiple communities. Hundreds of people would walk great distances every day to see the medical team. There were usually more people than could be seen each day, and on this particular day—their final day there—Steve's job was crowd control. They were in the community of Karima at a children's home called Tumaini (TOO-ma-EE-nee), which translates to "hope." He would ensure that people waited patiently before moving from triage to a doctor to the makeshift pharmacy. An animated young man approached Steve early in the day. He had traveled a long way on his bicycle just to convince Steve to visit his home. Steve graciously declined because he couldn't possibly leave the medical camp with the growing crowd of people eager to see a doctor, but the young man persisted.

The young man waited patiently the entire day, repeating his invitation to Steve. When the crowd started thinning, Steve agreed to visit his home. They put the young man's bicycle in the van and drove for about twenty minutes down a very rough Kenyan road in the pouring rain. As they arrived, the rain stopped. They arrived in Kwambekenya, where Boniface proudly gave Steve a tour of his new home, which had been funded by BigStuf. They spent several minutes talking about Boniface's family and community.

Knowing that I was looking for a rural community, for local leaders who would take ownership, and for a community that was cohesive enough that residents would actively engage in the solutions, Steve recommended that I consider visiting Kwambekenya. We arranged for an introduction with Boniface and other community leaders when I visited for the first time in the fall of 2006. The vision was taking shape, and as I sat across from Boniface and his peers, I felt both excited and apprehensive.

I was acutely aware that whether we liked it or not, our mere presence in the community was setting expectations. Those expectations had real consequences, good and bad, so we needed to get the blueprint right. We met leaders from a few other communities during that trip. Many showed promise, and it was clear that some just wouldn't work. Kwambekenya was one of three communities where we felt compelled to engage. We might not have known exactly how we were going to do it, but now we knew where and with whom.

With burgeoning relationships with communities in-hand, the need to garner support for our work was critical. Upon my return stateside, much of my time was spent on fundraising. I knew that we couldn't affect change in Kenya without financial support from the West. I also knew that we wouldn't be successful unless we changed the paradigm of how the West engaged the poor. We organized events called a Night for Africa featuring comedian Jeff Foxworthy and an appearance by the Daraja Children's Choir—an initiative born out of one of Lanny's convictions that more people in the US could be gripped by the needs in East Africa if they experienced the people and the culture on their own turf. The Daraja (Swahili for "bridge") Choir toured all over the US for the next several years and became a powerful platform to communicate our model.

The Daraja Children's choir was made up of eighteen to twenty-four different children each year who would travel for several weeks with teachers and tutors. They would lead worship in American churches and perform in elementary schools. It's been inspiring to see those kids complete secondary school and many go on to complete college or university. One young boy, a former street child in Nairobi whose life was spent stealing his next meal, foraging through urban trash piles, and sniffing glue to feel warm, was in a rehabilitation center when he expressed interest in joining the choir. Fourteen years later, through the help of 410 Bridge and generous sponsors, he has completed law school and is working as an attorney. There are many success stories like his, as nearly 150 former Daraja kids continue their journey of development.

The Night for Africa events and the Daraja Choir served as wonderful mouthpieces for our work in those early years. But we knew we needed personal, long-term relationships that would link those who *really* wanted to help on our side of the bridge with the people we were meeting in Kenya. We created a model for US donors and organizations to partner with Kenyan communities for the life of the 410 Bridge partnership; during the course of that relationship, we would send people, resources, and talents but, most importantly, enable relationships with the people in their sister community.

I was encouraged to find that so many people I talked to were eager to engage the poor in a different way. Many had already been through experiences similar to my Butalale trip: They were disillusioned. They didn't feel like they were making a *real* difference. They had no desire to give up on the effort but didn't know how to disrupt the status quo.

ESTABLISHING THE BLUEPRINT

In the midst of so many logistical considerations—travel plans, fundraising events, program management on the other side of the world, and choir tours for a couple dozen Kenyan children—I knew that we had to devote considerable time and effort to the theoretical foundation of 410 Bridge. If we were serious about disrupting the traditional approaches to poverty in developing communities, we needed a clear expression of our guiding principles and how those ideals translated to action. I had read a handful of books on the topic, but even as I gleaned some useful concepts from the authors, I found them more theoretical than practical.

To be honest, it was easier in those days to verbalize what we *didn't* want to do than what we *did* want to do. I knew, for example, that the men in Butalale should have been engaged with our school construction project, but I also knew that my first instinct—to grab the men I saw sitting around doing nothing and say, "What are you thinking?"—was probably not the most nuanced approach. My own Ugandan missteps, as well as research and experiences of others who had been frustrated by a lack of sustained change from well-intentioned efforts, had created a laundry list of *don'ts* with the way this all had been done for years.

We understood that Americans were too quick to push solutions of their own making, addressing problems that they had identified, and that those solutions frequently did little more than put a Band-Aid on a serious illness. We knew that efforts from the West lacked sufficient engagement from the beneficiaries—that writing checks, building schools, and digging wells was not the sum total of a poverty alleviation strategy. We understood, in fact, that most well-wishers in the West had not been operating strategically at all. Instead, they were operating from emotion or an attachment to pet projects that hampered local ownership and failed to prioritize sustainability. We knew that focusing on aid and relief created a pattern of unhealthy giving that undermined empowerment, independence, and local economic efforts.

Good people on both sides of the bridge, people who truly desired to see things change, had unknowingly conspired to create a dysfunctional system that needed disruption. The solution would require discipline, a refusal to acquiesce when things got hard, and a steadfast adherence to the principles we established. We knew we wouldn't do it perfectly, but we also knew that we wouldn't get anywhere near our destination if we didn't have a navigation plan before we embarked.

A key piece of that plan was erecting guardrails—nonnegotiables that would keep us in the lane as we proceeded. Our early guiding principles highlighted bedrock values like integrity, hard work, clarity of communication, and accountability. We didn't know how severely our foundation would be tested in the coming years; when you do something new, the gravitational pull inevitably tries to pull you back to the status quo. By setting up our guardrails and the navigational tools that would guide us no matter what, we tried to head off situations that were still miles down the road.

KEY QUESTIONS

The vision was to create community-driven solutions that would eventually be indigenously self-sustaining and communities that were compassionate, free, and prosperous, communities with dignity, purpose, and freedom. But how could we actually achieve that? Granted, it would take time—a long time. Communities needed water, roads, schools, medical facilities. They needed to learn how to move from insufficiency to self-sufficiency, to create businesses, to learn trades, and to motivate their neighbors. While the list of needs was long, we were committed to driving toward outcomes that would lead to a self-sustaining community. It was an ambitious goal that could happen only under the power of strong indigenous leaders.

We knew that every 410 Bridge community partnership would have a distinct beginning and a distinct end, and even if we couldn't define exactly what came in the middle, we started to formulate some questions that would guide us on each journey between a Kenyan community and a Western partner. Like the guiding principles, they were questions that would enable us to make decisions consistent with our identity, our values, and our mission. They were questions that would set our community interactions apart from those that had been established before us—questions like:

- What if we started with clear communication and mutually agreed upon outcomes?

- What if we figured out how to go a mile deep and an inch wide?

- What if we emphasized the resources that already existed in a community?

- What if we relied completely on local leadership?

- What if we cast the poor as the heroes of their own story?

- What if we made relationships the first priority?

The principles embedded in those questions would become our guide as we waded into the water with communities like Kwambekenya and Karogoto. If we *really* wanted to help, we needed to keep those questions at the forefront and, with discipline, aim for the outcomes they represented.

CHRIS'S STORY

Chris is one of my heroes. When he tells of the day he became an orphan at seventeen, he explains that he had only one day-to-day priority: putting food in his stomach. He was still grieving the loss of his mother, who had died suddenly as he was finishing his secondary school exams. His father was an alcoholic and had died of liver failure five years earlier. His two older sisters were married, living on their own, and caring for Chris's younger sister.

Chris felt completely alone because he was completely alone. He had no idea how to make a way in this world, so his only priority was to ensure that he had food in his stomach. He was just existing, living in the small rundown house where he had grown up. A couple times a week he might walk to a neighboring homestead where a friend of his family would hire him to tend to a small farm. Chris would ask for the little bit of work and make enough money to get the food he had prioritized. He was alone and still grieving. He didn't know where to turn, what to do, or how to move forward.

Then a friend named Dorcas, who worked as the 410 Bridge community coordinator in Kahuria, and Joseph, a member of the Kahuria Leadership Council, visited Chris to invite him to attend a training sponsored by 410. Chris asked what the class was about, and they replied simply, "Just come and see for yourself." Chris had literally nothing else to do and was sufficiently curious, so he showed up for the first day of what turned out to be a Business Start-Up Training (BST) class.

Even as an uncertain teenage orphan, Chris knew right away that he was in the right place. Micah Mwati, the instructor of the course

(Yvonne Busolo—410 Bridge)

Chris and his beautiful family.

and the economic development program coordinator for 410 Bridge, told Chris and his classmates that even if they didn't believe they had the resources to start a small business, they had everything they needed if they were breathing and healthy. Chris quickly found himself energized to make a better life for himself. "That day I said to myself, 'I am the man of my house. There's no other man in my family, so I must be the man and provide.'"

He kept attending every class and was usually the first one to arrive. Before the BST curriculum goes into any instruction of business principles, it builds a foundation by teaching the truths of the Christian faith—that in all things we must start with God. The training emphasizes the need to start with what God has already provided for you. Chris responded readily to God's work in his life. He made a commitment to follow Christ and to prioritize his faith in everything he did.

Micah took a special interest in Chris, often using him as an example in front of the class. The attention made Chris feel special. He remembers the day Micah asked him, "What do you do?" Chris said, "Why do you ask?" and Micah answered, "You look like a big businessman." It wasn't close to true yet, but when Micah spoke those words of encouragement into Chris, something deep inside him started to believe it. He learned how to relate to his neighbors—the people who would become his customers. He learned how to think of the world beyond filling his own belly, and he came to understand that as he made room for others, he would discover himself.

Chris got a temporary low-paying job so he could save enough to purchase a small television and a DVD player. He had a business idea—something that he felt was needed in Kahuria. He rented a small space in the town center and started charging admission for people to come and watch movies and recorded soccer games. Before he knew it, his theater was filling up, and he saved enough from that initial venture to buy a larger TV and a satellite dish, which allowed him to show live soccer games. His neighbors loved it, and his business thrived. But the theater was only the beginning of Chris's entrepreneurial efforts.

He planted potatoes on his property and started to sell them at market, making enough to buy a cow. Soon he was selling potatoes and milk, but his eye was constantly on ways to expand and upgrade his business. Since the market for potatoes and milk is flooded in Kahuria, he took classes teaching him how to make crisps (french fries) and yogurt, adding value to his resources and allowing for more profit. His goal was to become so successful with crisps and yogurt that he could hire some local youth to help him with the production.

With the profits from his farm and his theater, Chris tore down his old family home and built a new, larger home for himself and his young family—his new wife and his baby girl. When COVID-19 became a reality in Kenya and the government would not allow him to gather people in his makeshift theater, he reverted to his BST training and bought an incubator so he could hatch chicks for sale. And Chris had undertaken all those business ventures and personal improvements by the time he was twenty—just three years after his mother had passed and he became an orphan. More importantly, he did it without resources or seed capital from outsiders.

Today he supports his young family and pays his younger sister's school fees. He and the Kahuria Leadership Council see Chris as a mentor to idle youth in his community. Whenever he can, he reminds them of their potential to be productive businesspeople, offering to hire them for one of his ventures or rent them space in one of his incubators. He understands that he has a responsibility to set an example for the youth in Kahuria. In a village where many of the young people are relying on their parents, Chris—the young man who lost his parents—is a shining light for others around him who are struggling to find their way into responsible adulthood.

Joseph, the member of the Leadership Council who first invited Chris to the BST class and one of Chris's neighbors, puts it this way: "I knew him when he was still very, very young. Chris has been an eye-opener to many youths around our community. They envy him, and we help them recognize that if they like what Chris is doing, emulate him. Try to follow his footsteps. And by so doing, we'll have more people like Chris, a stronger community, with no one in Kahuria living in poverty."

CHAPTER THREE

In my transition from the for-profit sector to the nonprofit world, one of the most significant differences I noticed was the elevation of emotion in decision making. Our work with the extreme poor happens in a very emotional space, especially when it involves children. When emotions rise, the path toward strategic outcomes becomes blurred. Priorities and discipline become harder to manage when heartbreak takes over. Our mission and vision were clear, but values and guiding principles were needed to establish guardrails to avoid the natural gravitational pull toward *simply helping.*

Guiding principles are rooted in values. Values define our common ground. They allow organizations to define what they believe and the behaviors that will drive decisions in the midst of emotion, disagreement, or conflict. Guiding principles provide the guardrails needed to stay "on-mission." We hammered out an initial set of guiding principles as we sought to define what 410 Bridge was and what it wasn't. They've been refined over the years—and will continue to be refined—but since the beginning, we've had a set of guiding principles for the organization as a whole, our role in communities, and the role of US visitors.

We rise and fall on our definitions. Our guiding principles, therefore, needed to define key aspects of our mission. One of the bedrock guiding principles is our definition of *development.* Development is what people do for themselves. True development is not what outsiders do *for* people. Outsiders do projects. We may call them community *development* projects, but they're just that . . . projects. Communities living in poverty will embody development—what they do for themselves—when *they* lead, actively participate, and take ownership of their progress. If that paradigm was misunderstood by either side of the bridge from the outset, every subsequent step would take us further off course.

LEADERSHIP COMES FROM WITHIN

We learned early on the critical importance of entering a community well—properly framing expectations and having a clear understanding of what effective community development in extreme-poverty environments should look like.

The friends we were making on the other side of the bridge had their own expectations based on prior experiences with Westerners who had come over to help—people with big smiles, grand plans, and lots of money. These perspectives of the motives and practices of visitors from the West are deeply entrenched, and one of our persistent challenges is restructuring the thinking of our indigenous staff, the leaders in the communities, and the community members themselves. That process starts from the first meeting in a new community, and its success is linked to our absolute commitment to identify and strengthen indigenous leaders.

John Maxwell said it, and I couldn't agree more: "Everything rises and falls on leadership." If the needle were going to move, it would move and stay moved only because of strong indigenous leadership from the community and our staff. What benefit is it if when we leave a community—like so many others who have come and gone before us—there is no leadership capacity to encourage continued development? That's why indigenous leaders who have learned to lead well, who have earned the trust of their community, who understand what it means to self-develop, are key to starting, and finishing, well.

From the outset I've been committed to 100 percent indigenous in-country staff. I wanted Kenyans helping Kenyans, Haitians helping Haitians, and Guatemalans helping Guatemalans. In my view, the last thing our field staff needs is an American muddling up the works. This isn't always a popular perspective, especially among those who feel called to serve overseas or those who place a premium on avoiding risk. But for me, it's always been a nonnegotiable.

Despite the passionate disagreement around this principle over the years, I've gone to the mat on it. The case often made for American presence in country is founded in issues of finances, trust, and accountability. I get that. The way cultures think about money is very different. We can't remove ourselves from our Western way of thinking about money any more than we can take the chicken out of the chicken salad. But when it's our money that's going over there, we're often consumed by the prospect of loss of control or by the fear of the misappropriation of funds. These are reasonable concerns for sure, but in our quest for control we lose sight of the long play.

This principle is a complicated minefield, and despite the fact that one of those mines exploded in my face in 2010, I remain convinced that the downside of an American on staff is greater than the upside. When you insert an American into the in-country mix, it might help with communication and accountability from the Western perspective, but that person will be seen as an open channel of information back to the States. That leads to a lack of transparency, an erosion of trust, and an in-country team that never feels fully empowered to lead the effort. I've always seen trust as a choice. Sure, it can be earned (and lost), but in the end, we still make a choice to trust people or not. Our choice to trust and invest in our indigenous staff, let them lead their country offices, and give them the freedom to fail was fundamental.

And one of those failures—a big one—came in the summer of 2010. I received a phone call from our Kenya country director telling me that our staff controller had withdrawn all of our cash from multiple bank accounts and was on the run. My first reaction was disbelief, followed immediately by, "How could this happen?" We had appropriate controls in place that required multiple signatures on checks, so if she did this, she would have had to do it in collaboration with other staff leadership. We were audited by a third-party firm that verified controls and processes, yet a trusted member of our team, employed for multiple years, convinced one of her peers to break protocol, went to the bank with signed checks, and withdrew all of the funds that were being used to help the most vulnerable people living in her country.

What was even harder to fathom was that this individual grew up a sponsored child within a well-respected faith-based child sponsorship organization. She graduated at the top of her class, received a college education, and was invited into that organization's leadership development program. She came highly recommended by trusted people, and no one ever suspected that she could, or would, do such a thing. But she did.

She was ultimately found hiding in western Kenya and arrested. She was tried and convicted and spent time in jail. We never got the money back, and I doubt we ever will.

This was a difficult time in our history, and some would say that it could have been avoided had an American been running the show from inside Kenya. Perhaps, but we're not immune from greed and dishonesty. People are people. Temptations exist. Controls, as good as they may be, can be violated, and breaches of trust like the one we endured prompted us to make the accountability structures even stronger.

AN INVITATION TO HELP

The manner in which we enter a community today is very different from in the early days. Back then, our very first exposure to communities was through contacts we knew who knew community leaders. Friends of 410, who caught the vision of what we were trying to accomplish, forged introductions on our behalf.

Today, it takes more than just an introduction. We won't consider a new community unless we are formally invited by the community itself. Remember, the idea was to move the needle in a place to such a degree that the places around that place took notice and invited us in. That started happening fairly quickly. Neighbors talk. Word spreads quickly. I love hearing about leaders in our current communities, approached by their neighbors inquiring about the development they see happening, who tell them, "Don't expect 410 to come in and do anything for you. They do *with* us. If you think they are coming to do projects *for* you, you are wasting your time." What a welcome confirmation of a fresh way of thinking.

To clarify, doing *with* people and not *for* people doesn't mean our support is limited to verbal encouragement and "attaboys." Quite the contrary. We provide resources, lots of them, but only when the community shows initiative and participates in its development. After all, development is what people do for themselves. There are a variety of ways a community can participate: raising financial support, securing local government resources or permissions, donating land or infrastructure, providing labor, and more. Without community participation, we'd only be doing *for* people, and that's a nonstarter.

A powerful story that illustrates this point happened in Ngaamba. In most rural Kenyan communities like Ngaamba, access to safe water is usually the highest priority. People may walk hours every day to fetch their daily water from polluted rivers, ponds, or earthen dams. It's a huge problem that needs to be solved if we ever expect to build the capacity for self-development. Infrastructure water projects can be extremely expensive, and in communities where the people earn less than $2 a day, it's impossible to solve the problem without assistance from outsiders. But just because they need help from outsiders doesn't mean local people do nothing. They have to participate and take ownership of the solution.

One of the solutions presented by the leaders in Ngaamba was to distribute the water from a borehole to a subvillage some five kilometers away. The leaders proposed that if we could help with the pipes, the community would do the rest, and we agreed. The day they scheduled the work, the entire community came out, hundreds of people, to dig the trench and lay the pipes. Amazingly, they dug five kilometers of trench by hand and laid the pipes before lunch! Twelve years later, that water project continues to sustain itself without further assistance from outsiders. This type of community involvement is not uncommon. It's a source of pride to the community and a catalyst for continued self-development.

SETTING THE STAGE FOR A PARTNERSHIP

Once people from a new community contact our staff expressing an interest to form a partnership, our in-country leadership schedules an initial meeting to outline fundamental principles and expectations. Importantly, it's best if a *mzungu* (the Swahili word for a white person) isn't involved in those first meetings. I was involved in the early days, of course, but I quickly came to realize that when a mzungu shows up in the community, unhealthy expectations are set. No matter how hard we try, when we arrive in a community, the community sees dollar signs. Eliminating those expectations is critical to starting well. Don't get me wrong: I love participating in those meetings. I love meeting with the leaders and creating those relationships. It feels good. But another guiding principle—one that is extremely difficult for many do-gooders to grasp—is that we have to separate what we give, and how we give it, from our need to feel good about ourselves. If we were going to start well and set appropriate expectations, we needed to stay home and let our indigenous staff lead.

Ideally, our in-country leadership will explain that a partnership is predicated on the community's desire to self-develop. The word "partnership" is another one of those words that's inconsistently defined and often misused. We make it clear that we don't pay anyone for participating in the partnership and that we aren't going to take the lead on any initiative. We emphasize their need to be patient, pointing out that partnerships are long term in nature, have a high degree of mutuality, and are rooted in relationships between people on both sides of the bridge. Each side has responsibility in a healthy partnership, and if executed well, one plus one will equal something significantly more than two.

Occasionally, this initial meeting is the first and the last interaction we'll have. A few communities never formally invite us in or respond by sending us a list of project requests, which shows us that the people see outsiders as the solution to their problems. Most prospective communities, however, are enthusiastic about their development. Many have said that 410 is the first group to ask and listen. If the leaders want to move forward after that initial meeting, we ask them to write a formal invitation. The invitation is important, since it underscores the fact that the local community is taking the lead. They lead, we follow. After the official invitation is accepted, we move to the selection of the Leadership Council.

STEP ONE: THE RIGHT LEADERS

We take the quality of local leaders very seriously. The success of a partnership depends on the integrity, consistency, and intentionality of the people who represent their community.

There are two truths about leadership that have served us well. First, "Leadership abhors a vacuum," which means that the absence of leadership doesn't last long. The gap *will* be filled by someone. The question becomes whether or not that person is worthy of being followed. Too many times, we've been introduced to a self-appointed leader who simply stepped into the leadership vacuum and was incapable of really leading anything.

The second truth is "If you think you're leading but no one is following you, are you really a leader?" Being the loudest voice in the community doesn't amount to a whole lot if no one is following you. It takes time to cycle through those who think they are leaders (self-appointed), those who want to be leaders (aspirational), and those who have the most visibility (popular) in the village. If you want to find who the real leaders are in a community, consider how the community is organized: associations, churches, co-ops, savings groups, clubs, etc. Find the leaders of those groups and you will likely find who the people are following.

The Leadership Council ("LC"), which typically ranges from five to thirteen people, can be appointed or elected depending on the wishes of the community. We try to ensure that the LC represents all of the constituencies within the community, namely, the women, the youth, and the elderly. We encourage the LCs to institute term limits to inject new ideas and perspectives into the council and avoid corruption over time.

Not everyone who leads in the community is suited for a role on the LC. I'm painting with a broad brush here, but while pastors may be good teachers, shepherds, and effective leaders of a church, some aren't necessarily equipped to lead beyond their church walls. Similarly, school principals or head teachers can advocate tirelessly for their schools, but experience has taught us that they typically lack the perspective to broaden that concern to other areas in the community. And, most importantly, we learned the hard way that elected officials should not serve on the LCs. Politicians are not leaders. They have self-interests—like reelection—beyond the needs of the community.

LCs evolve and strengthen over time. One of the foundational principles that we communicate early and often, because it's yet another departure from the way things are typically done, is that serving on the LC is voluntary and unpaid. It's surprisingly common for NGOs to pay local people to serve in leadership roles or to attend meetings. I've heard the arguments for it, and I simply disagree. When local leaders are paid to attend meetings, a few unhealthy dynamics rear their ugly head. First, people attend because they're getting paid, not necessarily because they're capable leaders. Second, they are less likely to be candid with their new "employer," since a giver/receiver dynamic has been established. And, third, the barrier to effective leadership isn't financial. We want leaders who are ready, willing, and able to lead their communities—not because they're being paid but because they have a vision for their community and they want to lead that change.

Sadly, because of this misguided traditional approach, countless LC members have told us that many in their community don't believe that they are serving voluntarily. Our volunteer model is so different from the norm, and skepticism about Western handouts is so rampant, that we have to take extra care to be consistent with the "no pay" policy. Some LCs have requested something seemingly innocuous, like a provision for tea and bread for their meetings. We've tried to turn that around and ask them to involve their community. Why not ask the local churches to provide tea, especially if it will help support the people who are spending so many hours trying to chart a new course for the community? Again, we have to change the narrative from first seeking assistance outside the community to looking for solutions inside the community, no matter how small or seemingly insignificant.

It shouldn't be a surprise to anyone that every community everywhere includes crooked people hoping to enrich themselves in the name of public service. Our history has its share of bad actors who have, at times, even sabotaged a potential partnership for a needy community. One such situation happened years ago in Depatus, a community in the Laikipia region of Kenya. We know it as Segera.

THE ISSUE OF BAD ACTORS

We were invited to work in three communities in the Segera area: Depatus, Endana, and Ereri. Depatus is a desperately poor marketplace community. A brown bacteria-filled river runs through the center of town. Sanitation was nonexistent, and there was a desperate need for economic development and education. The other two neighboring communities had the same issues, with the exception of the water. In Ereri and Endana, access to any water was an hour's walk away. We were invited to meetings in Depatus, but the self-appointed leaders were toxic and demanding. They made collaboration impossible. They were completely self-serving, yet they wielded considerable influence over the people. They used that power to undermine our work, even bad-mouthing us to the nearby communities and government officials. Accusations against us of human trafficking, corruption, and bribery were common. It was frustrating to see the desperation in the eyes of the people and, at the same time, their unwillingness to recognize that their self-appointed leaders were one of the big reasons for their situation.

We proceeded cautiously. The Depatus leadership identified the lack of appropriate sanitation as a significant problem in their community. It's not uncommon in very rural areas for people to walk to the bush to "do their business." To help build trust in the early stages of our relationship, we agreed to engage a US team to help construct a few community pit latrines. A typical pit latrine is dug by hand ten to twelve feet into the ground, with a cement slab and a simple structure (outhouse) on the slab. The heat and altitude of this area of Kenya make the work hard and exhausting. The leaders agreed to mobilize the community to work with the team, but while the Americans were working, the local men just sat and watched. One of the Americans asked them why they weren't helping. The reply was disturbing: "Because we were told not to help you unless you paid us." Instead of the leadership encouraging the community to unite and solve some of their issues together, they undermined one of the first projects and set an unhealthy expectation for any future relationship.

As Bob Lupton said in his book *Toxic Charity*, "To do for others what they have the capacity to do for themselves is to disempower them." If we continued to construct the latrines while the community did nothing, we would do more harm than good. The team packed up for the day with hopes of coming back the next day with the locals joining them. Unfortunately, when they returned the next day, all of the tools had been stolen.

Over the years other organizations came to Depatus with offers to pay those same leaders to meet and plan projects. When it became evident that we weren't willing to line their pockets or elevate them in any way, they did what they could to undermine our credibility in the area. Today Depatus is stuck in the same place it was back then, while the two nearby communities where we partnered have graduated, are growing, and are sustaining their own development.

ORIENTATION THAT CHANGES THE NARRATIVE

Fortunately, for every nonstarter like Depatus there are plenty of encouraging places like Kwambekenya, our testing ground as we figured out how to execute our model in the early days, or Tumutumu, whose leaders invited us in after seeing the progress being made in their neighboring community of Karogoto. In those places, local leaders step up to serve solely out of a desire to make a difference. They have the vision, passion, and commitment to a better life for themselves and their neighbors, and through our training process we help them turn that vision into action. They are the heroes.

The orientation is designed to equip LC members to lead their community into a period of sustained change. We let them

Kwambekenya's first Leadership Council.

know that the three priorities of the LC are to be a voice for their entire community, to establish the development priorities, and, most importantly, to mobilize and unify the community to do for themselves. We kick off our relationship by redirecting the conversation from where it typically starts. Most people and organizations start the conversation with "How can I help you?" or "What do you need?" In my view, those are the wrong questions, and they kick the relationship off in the wrong direction. We have less interest in learning about their needs and more interest in learning about their vision. Where do they want to go? What do they dream about? How do they hope to realize their vision? But vision looks to the future, and that's a difficult concept for a culture like Kenya that, believe it or not, doesn't even have a word for "future."

Early on, one of my favorite questions to ask leaders was, "Imagine your community five to ten years in the future as completely transformed: tell me what you see." I came to learn that challenging leaders to imagine the future, and then asking them to paint a verbal picture of what they imagine, casts significant doubt in their minds about my sanity. After all, they live day-to-day. Tomorrow will take care of itself. For someone to ask them to imagine five, ten, twenty years into the future is, to them, literally crazy.

So, while we still ask that question, we had to change the narrative. We needed to put the focus squarely where it should be: on the assets, skills, and resources around them. Instead of starting with their problems, we begin with "What do you love about your community?" and "Tell us why someone would want to live here."

These simple questions begin to change the thinking from external (outside their community) to internal (inside their community).

PUSHING A ROPE

The training has evolved over the years, but in our first community and our twentieth, we've always sought to remind the LC that they are the architects and owners of any improvement plans for their community, that we are there only to do things *with* them but never *for* them. In 2007 a group of 410 representatives that included me and a few of our early Kenyan staff sat down with the newly established Kwambekenya LC to launch our first partnership. In a simple illustration that made an important point, I brought a long piece of rope with me. I gave one end of the rope to one of the local leaders, held onto the other end, and stretched it out across the room. Then I asked, "This rope represents our partnership. If we try to push you, how far will we go together?" Laughter filled the room as I began to push the rope and the leader at the other end of the rope went nowhere. "But," I continued, "if you pull us (you lead), and we want to follow you (you're a good leader), we can go a long way together."

My newfound friend pulled on his end, pulling me along as he moved, demonstrating his eagerness to lead and for us to follow. This is a simple but critical illustration of the right relationship between the local community and the West. As the leader guided me around the room, the other leaders nodded. What I didn't fully grasp at the time, but have been told repeatedly since, was the level of gratitude and relief that the leaders felt from this approach. They were excited (and relieved) that a Western organization was there to help by *asking*, not telling. Too many times, the West enters uninvited and starts talking about all the problems that they (the West) see as needing to be fixed. After all, the problems are so obvious to us, right? I mean, anyone spending an hour in the community can see the problems, right? Answering those questions in the affirmative only serves to place our priorities ahead of theirs.

To flesh out that shift in perspective from the outset of our LC orientation, we take every LC through a process called asset mapping. For people whose only previous interaction with do-gooders has been receiving handouts or watching when mission teams swoop in to put up a new building, paint a church, or run their version of a VBS, the asset-mapping process represents a profound reframing of what development means. It is designed to show local leaders that they have more tools, resources, and giftings than they think they have—resources they can use to change their lives and the lives of their neighbors.

Much of our approach has been adapted from my friend Dr. Ravi Jayakaran. We start by asking what they love about their community, pressing them to list in detail what is special about where they live. They might say things like, "We have good soil and a climate conducive to growing things," "We have strong churches," "We have good leaders," or "We are a unified, hard-working people." We write all of those positive attributes down and post them on a wall.

Next, we ask them to list the individual skills, gifts, and talents of the people living in their community. "What do your people do so well that they could teach others?" They create a detailed inventory of the craftspeople, farmers, entrepreneurs, and others living among them who have something valuable to offer, and that list goes on the wall as well. Then we move to assets that exist inside their community: a river may wind through the community, or they may have a primary school, a marketplace, or a dispensary. And, finally, we ask them to identify assets outside their community but near enough for them access. Examples could be a large marketplace in the next community over, a hospital that residents can reach via public transportation, or a water project in a neighboring village. Those assets are written down and hung up with the others, creating a visual display that allows LC members to initiate their partnership with a firm grasp of the things in their community that they could leverage for good without any outside assistance.

In seeking to tilt the community's outlook toward the positive, we aren't denying that problems exist. The local leaders wouldn't have invited us to their community if they didn't have serious issues that needed to be addressed. But because of prior perceptions of how outside do-good organizations usually operate, they are likely to enter those first sessions focused on their problems and deficits, not their strengths and gifts. By moving assets to the beginning of the conversation—by sharing the positive attributes of their people—we begin to change their focus and set them up to see the tools they already have in their toolbox to solve the problems that they want to solve.

TEN USEFUL SEEDS

After the LC members thoroughly outline their community's strengths, they're ready to move to the assessment phase. Our assessments leverage a simple but effective technique called the Ten Seeds Technique. Developed by Dr. Jayakaran, the Ten Seeds Technique is a simple and ingenious approach to creating a visual representation of a community's situation and goals. It bridges language barriers and allows participants to engage in an interactive discussion about important issues.

We use the Ten Seeds Technique for a variety of assessment questions like age distribution, preventable diseases, sources of income, and water resources. In all, we may assess a community across twenty to thirty different criteria, not necessarily to measure definitive data but to build a baseline of how the community views itself.

One of the most telling assessment exercises that illustrates how the Ten Seeds Technique works is Income Classification. We start this exercise by asking the leaders for the word or phrase in their native language that best describes "the rich"—the people who have plenty. Culture and local language are important, so we want to use their words, not ours, to ensure an accurate and common understanding. We continue by asking for the word or phrase for people who have enough plus a little left over. They're not "the rich," but they have some extra every month. We then move to the word or phrase for people who have enough but don't have any extra. And we finish with the word or phrase for people who do not have enough for their basic needs. Then we give them ten seeds (coffee beans, maize kernels, or small stones). The ten seeds represent 100 percent of their community. We ask them to distribute the seeds across the four income levels to give us a sense of how many people are in each income class.

The important conclusion drawn from the Income Classification assessment isn't how many people are rich or poor or somewhere in between. The point is to learn how the com-

Population Ratio	Local Name (& Description)
	Matajiri (the well off)
	Nafuu ("somehow manage")
	Mutsowi ("they lack")
	Mkiya ("poor")

munity perceives itself. From there, we ask them to think about the highest level of education for each income category. We isolate each income level and ask the leaders to represent that group's furthest level of education using the ten seeds.

It isn't necessary to capture assessment data with perfect accuracy. Again, what we're trying to learn is the community's perception of itself. In the example to the right, we see that while the rich account for only a small percentage of the population, they are the best educated. In this example, the community perceives itself as predominantly poor and uneducated. Whether they are or are not is less important than the reality that they *think* they are.

Most of the time, regardless of the country, 60 to 80 percent of the seeds are in one of the two poorest categories. When we break those down related to levels of education, they are able to see clearly, based on their own assessment, that the poorest people

Population Ratio	Local Name (& Description)	Furthest Level of Education Achieved				
		Some Primary	Completed Primary	Some Secondary	Completed Secondary	Tertiary
	Matajiri (the well off)				🫘🫘🫘	🫘🫘🫘
	Nafuu ("somehow manage")			🫘🫘🫘	🫘🫘🫘	
	Mutsowi ("they lack")		🫘🫘🫘	🫘🫘	🫘	
	Mkiya ("poor")	🫘🫘🫘🫘🫘🫘🫘				

among them have had the most limited educational opportunities. It's an interactive exercise that gets them to start visualizing where to focus their attention. Most importantly, they start thinking about desired outcomes (higher household incomes and quality education for all children), not just projects like school buildings.

MINING FOR CONFLICT

The most productive, and interesting, assessment sessions happen when the at-large community members are in the room when the leaders go through the assessment process. In Kawira—an early community partnership that did not succeed—we probably should have seen the broader problem with the leadership before we actually did, but about seventy-five community members were packed into an adjacent classroom as the newly appointed LC was working through the assessments. Every time the leaders would tackle an assessment category like the one illustrated earlier, we presented their assessment to the at-large community to get their take on the leaders' answers. Many laughed or just shook their heads in disapproval. A lively discussion ensued, and community members challenged the leaders.

At first it was just some lighthearted ribbing. We saw it as a healthy discussion with varied perspectives, but in short order it became clear that the community had a very different outlook on the realities in their community than what the leaders were sharing. The at-large community members, not being in a position of leadership or being the voice of their community, revealed that the leadership was out of touch, ignorant of the realities, or, more likely, telling us what they thought we wanted to hear.

I always find it fascinating when community members, even after recognizing that their leaders do not represent them well, stick with the same leaders. They have an opportunity to hold them accountable, change leadership, or step into a leadership role themselves, but they resist. Cultural dynamics are largely at play here, and I get that. This is another reason why we encourage term limits and subcommittees that include community members who aren't on the LC. We want to expose more than the self-appointed to opportunities for leadership. Everything does, in fact, rise and fall on leadership, and Kawira was no exception. The leaders continued to represent their community poorly. Self-interests and power plays continued for a couple of years, and the partnership ultimately dissolved.

Up to this point in the training, we seek to shine a bright light on the solutions that exist *inside* a community—the leaders, the physical assets, and the giftings. We're also creating a baseline for how the community perceives itself. It's vital that the LCs develop a thorough inventory of the place they might have lived all their lives but never really assessed before. From there, the table is set to identify and prioritize the greatest challenges they face, through a sobering lens of how *they* intend to tackle those challenges. If we *really* want to help, all of these previous exercises set the table to introduce a critical principle: empowerment.

ESTHER'S STORY

When she was in the sixth grade at Kiu Primary School, Esther starting hearing bits of conversation that seemed too good to be true. People in her community were saying that 410 Bridge was starting a secondary school sponsorship program for top students from her school. These sponsorships, she heard, would help her parents cover some of the prohibitive costs of secondary school. She knew it was true, but even so, such an idea was, to her, a fantasy.

Esther had hopes for herself. When she was very small, she dreamed of becoming a doctor, but even as a young child, she could sense doors closing on that dream. In fourth grade, when she looked around her family's homestead, she would find herself getting discouraged. At one time her family had cows, goats, and chickens—which represented modest wealth in that agrarian society. But Esther tells the story of coming home from school one day and realizing that every cow, goat, and chicken had been sold over time to send her six brothers to a secondary school. Esther was the only one left at home, and she was faced with the reality that her family didn't have anything left to ensure that she could follow her brothers' path.

Secondary school is the equivalent of high school in the US, but the best schools operate as boarding schools, which are expensive and a long distance from the village. Every eighth grader in Kenya takes an important standardized placement test (KCPE) *at the end of the term, and the results of that test dictate the type of secondary school they get to attend. If they score below a certain level, their education essentially ends. Even if they perform well on the test, many can't afford to go away to school, and they must settle for lesser-quality local district schools or day schools.*

A door of hope opened slightly for Esther in class six, when she heard of the potential sponsorship opportunity for the best performers. She was painfully aware that the competition for these limited sponsorships would be intense. She committed to doing the hard work. She rose at 5 a.m. every day to study and help her mother around the homestead before making the forty-five-minute trek to school. Upon arrival, she would help prepare the classroom, find a textbook to do her homework, and help her teachers get ready for the day. She would attend class from 8 a.m. to 5 p.m., stay after school to work on math with a friend, and return home after 6 p.m. to help her mother prepare the evening meal. She'd do her chores, study next to a kerosene lantern, and go to bed. This routine continued for three years.

She confidently says that she felt she did everything she could to prepare for her KCPE placement exam. She knew that only two secondary school sponsorships were available, and she thought it was highly unlikely that she could finish at the top of her class. When the results came back, Esther had the third-highest score. Two boys scored ahead of her. She was devastated and told her mother that she was resigned to attend the district school near their home and shelved any earlier professional aspirations since they represented career paths that were usually closed to students at the less rigorous schools.

But then came a Sunday Esther will never forget, one that she characterized as "a special case of God's grace." She learned that the 410 leaders in Kiu had decided that they would grant sponsorships to the top-performing boy and girl in the community. Esther was the top-performing girl and received the sponsorship. Nearly ten years later, she still beams when she remembers receiving the news that she would receive a coveted sponsorship.

But this presented a new challenge for Esther. She was afraid that her community would see her sponsorship as unearned since she didn't perform in the top two spots, so she committed to doing the hard work in secondary school to prove that she was worthy of the investment.

With the sponsorship covering her tuition, room, and board, and her parents covering the cost of supplies and incidentals, Esther was enrolled in a higher-level secondary school, where she surprised her teachers by finishing first in her class of more than one hundred students. She was more economically challenged than most of her classmates. Unlike many of them, she came from a small rural village, and when it came to speaking English, she felt inferior to many of the students from more urban backgrounds. But a defining moment for her was when she realized that by doing the hard work, she could compete with, and even outperform, her classmates. She continued to excel all the way through secondary school, and when she finished, she arrived at another crossroads.

University would be economically impossible for Esther's family, but once again an unexpected door opened in the form of a college grant sponsored by the Kenyan government. Esther applied and was accepted, and in 2021 she was nearly finished with her degree in information technology and preparing for a career in networking. She was excited to see where her education could take her in the computer world—but even at twenty-three Esther had a separate ambition, one that sprung from the opportunity she had earned at the age of fourteen.

She wants to be part of helping other young people realize the opportunity that is before them. Every chance she gets, she tells primary *school students that they can do more than they ever dreamed but that they have to "do the hard work." She considers herself a mentor in her community, but her desire to make a difference extends far past Kiu, as I learned when I asked her about her plans for the future.*

Without hesitation, Esther looked me in the eye and said, "I want to be the next Kurt, of course. I want your job!"

CHAPTER FOUR

Every step of LC development is designed to put community change squarely into the hands of local leaders—to walk them through the process of understanding their assets and their struggles and to remind them that they can craft solutions inside their community without first seeking them from the outside. The assessments and evaluations lead us to the most interesting element of the Ten Seeds exercise—the Empowerment Analysis— once again adapted from our friend Dr. Jayakaran.

Everyone talks about empowerment. We wave the flag of empowerment as the ultimate solution and are quick to point to the lack of empowerment as a foundational problem in the fight against poverty. You won't hear any disagreement here. But once again, the tricky part is to move from being a flag-waving "fan" of empowerment to a pragmatic discussion about how empowered people really feel and how they actually affect change.

After the baseline assessments are completed, the big elephant in the room hasn't been discussed. The community has challenges.

Big ones. They have significant problems that they can't solve without assistance. Up to this point in the LC development sessions, we've intentionally *not* discussed their needs. To get that ball rolling, we ask every individual in attendance—leaders *and* community members—to identify what they see as the most pressing priority for the community. We ask that they do this privately—no groupthink here. We ask them not to discuss their response with anyone else. We want to know what they, as a single community member, see as the community's greatest challenge.

Some in attendance want to identify multiple challenges because, in their mind, there are several issues that need to be resolved. Solving just one of them won't make a difference, and they're right. Nonetheless, if they could change just one thing in their community, just one, what would they change? We urge them not to concern themselves with the barriers to change but simply to share the most important thing, in their individual opinion, that needs to change in the community. If they struggle, we may frame it using the next generation as the object. We say, "Think about your children or your grandchildren. What is one challenge that exists in your community today that you would hope your children or grandchildren would not have to experience?"

After everyone writes down their individual priority, we go around the room and ask them to reveal and explain their answer. Answers rarely vary from what one would expect. Challenges like access to safe water, education, employment, income opportunities, and health are among the most common. After everyone has shared their individual response, we ask them to work as a group to gain consensus on the single greatest priority. This often takes some time because people are passionate about *their* "one thing." Agreement may or may not come easily, but until they can work through their differences and settle on the most important issue, we allow them the struggle.

After they pinpoint their number one need, we talk about high-level solutions. What do they see as the solution to this major problem? Once again, we ask them not to focus on the barriers to the solution but simply to explain what *they* think the solution might be. For example, if access to safe water is their top priority, they might dream about a water purification system to clean the water flowing in a nearby river. They may have a solution for their local primary school to reduce congestion and improve the quality of education. In every case, they already have an idea of what the solution could be. Our job is to allow them to ideate around solutions that they develop on their own.

We listen to their ideas, gain a good understanding of what they think could be done, and then draw three concentric circles. The center circle represents the amount of their solution that they believe the community can do on its own. The next ring moving outward (middle ring) represents the amount of the solution requiring help from outsiders. And the outer ring is the amount of the solution that they believe is beyond anyone's control—drought, or a natural disaster, or it's up to God or the gods. We then hand over the ten seeds. We explain that these ten seeds represent 100 percent of their *solution* to their priority. We ask them to distribute the seeds across the three concentric circles. The diagram below illustrates a typical response.

One of the many dynamics I didn't understand when I led the early assessment exercises, but one I'm very much on the lookout for today, is the tendency for local leaders to tell us what they think we want to hear. Case in point, in our example above the LC now has a problem. They may hesitate about where to put the seeds, worrying that if they put too many seeds in the center ring, we may conclude that the community doesn't need our help. If they put too many seeds in the middle ring, they risk that we see them as helpless—unable to do enough on their own—and, once again, we may choose not to help. And if they put too many seeds in the outer ring, we may see them as hopeless and, again, choose not to help.

As they work through this exercise, we refer them to the asset mapping we did earlier. We encourage them to provide an honest assessment of their ability to contribute to the change that's needed, but their concern about how we will react can still get in the way of transparency.

When this exercise is finished, the LC members typically place two or three seeds in the center (their independent effort), six or seven in the middle (assistance from outsiders), and one in the outer ring (outside of anyone's control).

When they've made their final placement of the ten seeds, they're often surprised by our response. In their mind, they may feel that they've found a good balance that illustrates their desire to do *something* while highlighting an appropriate level of assistance from outsiders. If, as illustrated in the example above, they place three seeds in the center, the question often surprises them. We simply ask, "If you can do 30 percent of this solution on

Outside of anyone's control

Need help from outsiders

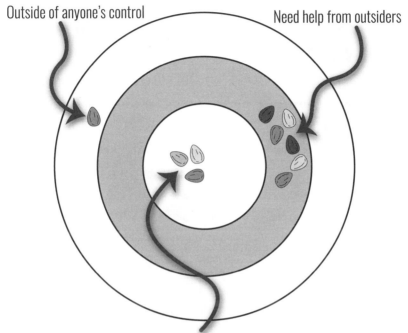

Community can do on their own?

your own, what are you waiting for?" We point to the assets that they listed now hanging on the wall—assets that exist inside and outside their community. We point to the strengths and talents of the people and the community as a whole. "If all of these great things and all of these assets exist within the community, why are you waiting for outsiders to come before you begin to solve these problems on your own?" And then we let them wrestle with the answer.

WHO GETS A RIDE?

We share a well-known African anecdote of two men who are each looking for a ride from their village to the city. One of them is sitting inside his home waiting for someone to come and give him a ride. The other is already walking to the city. We ask the leaders which man they would be more likely to assist. The answer, of course, is the man who is already on his way.

"What are you waiting for? Are you waiting for outsiders to come in before you begin working toward a solution?" These questions are not typically asked by Western do-gooders because too often we see ourselves as the solution to their problems. We have money, ideas, and solutions that they need. We have a love affair with efficiency and, frankly, want them to just step aside while we come to the rescue to solve their problems quickly. So, these questions, as blunt as they might be, begin to plant seeds for a paradigm shift in thinking. We help them understand that the problems that exist in their community don't exist in our community. And the solutions to their problems don't exist in our community either.

The other important question is this: "Who are these *outsiders*? Who are you hoping will come along from the outside to help you?" They may never have even contemplated that question. After all, these aren't small, insignificant problems. These are the biggest challenges they face in their community. It's more likely that they don't see themselves as *capable* of solving such a problem on their own, so the only other option must be *someone else*.

To help them think through it, we present more questions. Are they waiting on the local government to prioritize their community over their neighboring villages who suffer from the same issues? Are they waiting for some unnamed specialized NGO working in their country to swoop in to help them? Who exactly are these outsiders, and why should they want to help them?

We encourage them to consider the importance—as leaders—of being an advocate for their community. If *they* aren't going to advocate for change, who is? Have they approached their local government for assistance or sought out other NGOs to help them? Or, more likely, do they see 410 Bridge as the outsider they need because we happen to be here at this moment? If they're simply waiting for the government, or an organization like 410 Bridge, to show up and begin working, they are no different from the man sitting in his home waiting for someone to give him a ride to the city.

These discussions begin to change the paradigm of how they perceive their empowerment. The hard work is yet to come, but our goal is to set appropriate expectations and begin the long journey of the community embracing their empowerment and self-development because, once again, development is what people do for themselves.

A SMOOTHER ROAD

As we meet with new leaders in these communities, we try to communicate clearly in the hopes that they catch the vision for what we are trying to impart: that they will see substantive change only when they garner their own resources and work together toward a goal that they identify. This process can be so transformative that sometimes the empowerment analysis alone is enough to move the needle without any further intervention from us. This was the case when we were invited to help another organization mobilize a community in Honduras.

The asset-mapping process revealed that this Honduran mountain village had resources; they grew produce on fertile farmland and had plenty of livestock and dairy farming. They had ample exports to sell, but transporting them down the mountain was a problem.

We had completed much of the assessment process. The room was packed with fifty or more residents as we moved through the concentric circle empowerment analysis. There was almost no debate about the community's most pressing need. The twelve-kilometer road to and from their mountain village to the main road was in terrible shape. It could be navigated only by four-wheel-drive vehicles, so wholesale buyers would not dare make the journey up or down the mountain to purchase the community's commodities. That created a major barrier to the profits that they could take in from the sale of their produce and dairy products.

Everyone agreed that grading the twelve kilometers of mountain road was the number one priority. They went through the Ten Seeds Empowerment Analysis and concluded that they could do 40 percent of the work themselves but they needed outside assistance for the other 60 percent. As we navigated the discussion about identifying viable outsiders and being an advocate for their community, they began to identify local government offices that could partner with them and stand in the gap of what they couldn't do on their own.

The people were skeptical about their ability to petition authorities to get the funding they needed. Like most communities, they see the government as corrupt and self-serving. But several weeks after we left, with the energy that comes from community consensus, a couple hundred community members traveled down the mountain to approach the mayor with a solution. They explained that they were willing to mobilize their community, provide the labor, purchase the fuel, and hire an operator if the mayor would supply the heavy equipment needed to grade the road. To their surprise, he agreed, and the road was repaired within several weeks! When we returned to the community, they expressed their gratitude for the encouragement to change their thinking. They realized that they were, in fact, empowered to be advocates for their village and all of it happened because the community began to think differently about their role in the solution.

The orientation and planning process in those early meetings usually sparks plenty of enthusiasm to start the work, but we know from experience that the LCs will hit obstacles. And just as we emphasize that any forward progress must come from within the community, so, too, we resolve to let them labor through their leadership challenges from within.

It's critical that we let local leaders wrestle through the development process. Watching them struggle through seemingly simple problems, however, often sparks the West's emotions and misplaced sense of urgency and skews our judgment. When well-meaning outsiders see people already living in poverty hit a roadblock, their natural inclination is to jump in and fix the problem. In the West, time has authority. Our love affair with efficiency drives our desire to see progress and see that progress on our time line. Time and efficiency become the priority—especially when Western funding is involved—and we lose the discipline to allow the leaders to lead, to wrestle with indigenous solutions, and, yes, to possibly fail. An integral part of letting them lead their own work is allowing it to unfold at their pace and understanding that interruptions, delays, and missteps are an important part of the empowerment process.

THROUGH THE STRUGGLE TO A SOLUTION

We let one of our early Kenyan communities, Ngaamba, wrestle through a solution to their water problem, and the community was stronger for it. Ngaamba is in a semiarid region of Kenya. It is almost always dry, but in times of drought it is especially difficult. Water is life.

When our partnership began, Ngaamba had an old water project in disrepair. It was constructed decades before we arrived. The system was antiquated, but we helped the community restore the project, providing safe water once again. For several months, the community members had been paying for water under the oversight of a legacy water committee, not affiliated with or under the authority of the 410 Bridge LC. The legacy water committee was a small group of self-appointed managers who were theoretically responsible for all aspects of the project. As will happen, the system broke, and water stopped flowing. The money intended for repairs and maintenance was, not surprisingly, "misappropriated" by the members of the legacy water committee.

Enter 410 Bridge, which to Ngaambans looked like the cavalry coming over the hill to save the day. When we inquired why the water system was offline, they told us that the pump needed a replacement part. The part was small and readily available, but it cost about 10,000 Kenyan shillings ($200 USD at that time) to replace. We surveyed the situation and saw that the impact on the community of the broken water system was serious. People were forced to return to walking very long distances to gather polluted water from a seasonal river. They requested that we replace the part, so I asked the LC chairman to organize a meeting of local leaders for the next day.

About one hundred people showed up for the meeting. I was pleased with the turnout. When we got started, I asked a few questions. "How many people does this water project serve?" They told me about five thousand people. "How have they been getting water since the system stopped functioning?" They said that they had been walking a long way to the river, but the water was unsafe. They emphasized that people were getting sick and children were not attending school so they could gather water. They reiterated their request: they were desperate, and they were looking to us for the solution.

It wouldn't have been difficult for us to help. It wasn't about the money; I had more than what they needed in my pocket. But that wasn't the point. If the people tasked with maintaining the water project had selfishly abandoned their duty to serve their own motives, and if the other leaders and residents couldn't work to get this very important system up and running again for the health of their neighbors, assistance from us wouldn't get to the heart of what was really broken. If we put a Band-Aid on the problem, that wound would inevitably open up again, and they'd be looking to us for every Band-Aid thereafter.

I asked them one more question: "If five thousand people will use the water system and it costs ten thousand shillings, are you telling me that each person can't contribute two shillings to restore the water?" That was a tiny amount of money, even to those who didn't have much. But again, it wasn't about the money. It was about ownership.

One man leapt up and passionately argued his case. He explained that because of drought, the community hadn't had a meaningful harvest in two years and the poverty in the area was severe. The people were too poor to pay two shillings. Besides, he explained, the five thousand people included children, so it was more like one thousand households using the water. Even ten shillings per household was a small price to pay, I countered. But he continued to vigorously argue that families were too poor to solve this problem and it was incumbent upon us to help.

I thanked the man for his perspective and addressed the crowd. "Look, this is not our water project; this is Ngaamba's water project," I said. "The water problem that exists in your community doesn't exist in my community, and the solution to your water problems doesn't exist in my community either." The man started to respond, but then a member of the LC walked over and graciously sidled him back to his seat. The LC member apologized and said that their friend was embarrassing their community by insisting that they couldn't gather the resources for the replacement part. They confessed that it wasn't because the people didn't have the ten shillings; after all, it was a very small amount to collect from each household. The issue was that they saw the repair of the water system as the responsibility of outsiders, since outsiders originally built it. It wasn't that the people couldn't or wouldn't contribute to the solution. It was that the leaders didn't see it as their responsibility to look inwardly for the solutions first. After all, they had always looked to outsiders in the past.

Before long, the residents had gotten together and collected the money to get their water system working again. They also navigated the power dynamics to replace the legacy water committee with trustworthy people. It was a solution powered by unity, and it would never have occurred if we had failed to exercise a little tough love when Ngaamba had come to us looking for help. We are almost obsessive at times about communicating expectations clearly and making sure that the ball stays in the local community's court, even when they really want to toss it back our way. The discipline in sticking to our guiding principles leads to success stories like the one in Ngaamba—victories that the local people can rightfully claim as their own.

And, oh, by the way . . . all of Ngaamba's water projects have been indigenously sustained for over ten years.

ABOUT THOSE MISTAKES

With fifteen years of hindsight from the establishment of that inaugural partnership in Kwambekenya, I often say that we've gotten more wrong than we've gotten right. In 2021, I had the opportunity to sit down with a few of my friends in Kwambekenya—former LC members—to talk about the good, the bad, and the ugly from those early days. I was able to apologize for some things that we would have done differently today, but I was heartened to see that their commitment to unity and empowerment—grown and fostered over the years—is still driving them to work for the good of their community today.

One of our flashier mistakes (go big or go home, right?) came when we decided to launch the Kwambekenya partnership with a big celebration on the grounds of Kiambariki Primary School. Don't get me wrong; it was a fun day, attended by five thousand locals and dozens of Americans. We slaughtered and roasted several bulls, prepared hundreds of pounds of rice, and baked ten thousand chapati for the people who came.

But here's the thing. That big launch party in 2007 illustrates a theme that we see over and over again when Western efforts miss the mark. Our motives were fine. It was my idea, and all I wanted to do was kick off this exciting partnership in a memorable way that would involve the whole community. We wanted to celebrate with our new friends—to rally and demonstrate people from both sides of the bridge coming together to accomplish something meaningful. But with that massive event, we managed to propagate the idea that when the *wazungu* come to town, they bring the money with them. They come with lots of free food and a flashy party. My recent visit with my Kwambekenya friends left us all laughing embarrassingly at my misguided idea. They looked at me, shook their heads, and said as only a friend can say, "Bad idea, my friend. Bad idea." None of that, however, changed the fact that our Kwambekenya partnership was rooted in local leaders holding the reins. They led well and overcame our missteps.

Another noteworthy stumble from our early days will make you wonder whether I really learned my lesson in Butalale. When our first teams visited Kwambekenya, they (like the Kandler family in Butalale) wanted to bring a "second bag" of clothes to leave in the community. I hadn't completely forgotten about our experience in Butalale, so we adjusted the plan to allow the second bags to be left with the leaders. They would determine who in the community needed the team's generosity, and the wazungu wouldn't distribute the gifts directly. But it was a bad idea, nonetheless. A really bad idea.

For one thing, the pressure placed on the leaders was intense. There were never enough clothes for everyone who needed or wanted them, so all we did was delegate the same dynamic we experienced in Butalale to the leaders. It still fostered division rather than unity. It still stripped people of their dignity. And it created a very unhealthy expectation for the next set of Americans to visit Kwambekenya.

And there's the other unintended consequence with our desire to share "free stuff." I've met many entrepreneurs in communities who sell clothing and shoes in the local market, building their small retail businesses one clothing item at a time. When Westerners swoop in with piles of free clothes and shoes, it doesn't take a business genius to know what happens to the demand for clothing in a small community. I cringe to think how we negatively impacted entrepreneurs.

This is why it is *extremely* rare for visitors who come with 410 to give anything away. Nothing. Almost never. Like so many of our guiding principles, people disagree—sometimes vehemently. Some patterns have been so deeply established through the history of Western do-gooders that they aren't easily disrupted. The idea of giving things to the poor is one of them.

I can't count the number of times that Americans simply refuse to abide by our policy on giving stuff away. They ignore it and leave their clothes or shoes or money or whatever behind. They'll do it secretly, and if caught, they'll pitch the "I've been blessed to be a blessing" line or play the "God told me to do it" card.

I understand. I really do. I had a similar perspective in Butalale. But I didn't know better at the time. Now we do, and we are very clear. We don't allow visitors to give anything away. If someone from Butalale had told me why it was a bad idea and asked that I not do it, I would have listened and respected their position. Ignorance is one thing. Knowingly disregarding the negative consequences is another. The reality of the "I've been blessed to be a blessing" narrative is that because the *giver* isn't in need of what they're giving away, they view the receiver in a lesser light, perpetuating the victim/savior complex that does more to disempower people than empower them.

And another mistake worth noting: Shortly after our arrival in Kwambekenya, we added another guiding principle of what *not* to do. We would no longer build individual homes for pastors or community members like we did for Boniface. The only exception to this principle is in the event of a catastrophic event like a fire, hurricane, or earthquake. We discovered that unity is a tremendous catalyst for change, and if Westerners appear to help one pastor, or one family, over another, it can cause division and jealousy, undermining the very unity and cooperation that we're trying to foster. It can also lead to prioritizing self-interest over the needs of the community. It is disappointing when we visit a community and see that the nicest home in a community is the one belonging to the individual who has befriended a benefactor in the US.

Individual projects for specific households are still possible. In fact, we've built homes for families over the years but rarely and under unique circumstances. First, the community itself (usually the local church) must recommend and prioritize the individual need. Examples are for the most vulnerable in the community—a widow-led or child-led household or a family with a special-needs situation or perhaps a home that was destroyed by a catastrophic event or other special circumstance. This is usually because community members are burdened by their neighbor's hardship and want to help ease a tough situation. Second, they must be willing to help build it. If they recommend it and agree to help build it, we will consider helping. The point is this: the decision to build something for an individual family should not be based on an outsider's perception of need or an outsider's desire to assist; it must come from within the community itself. In the end, there is healthy pride of ownership because the community was part of the solution.

Through tapping strong local leaders and collaborating with them through the LC training process, we bear witness to a significant shift in the way people in 410 communities think about their circumstances and the solutions to their problems. It's amazing to watch capable leaders mobilize and empower their neighbors to institute authentic change in their communities, on their own. We hope that once Westerners see that change take place, they'll leave their emotions on the bus and resist undoing any of that progress by giving away a bag of free stuff.

But as meaningful as guardrails, guiding principles, strong indigenous leadership, asset mapping, community assessments, and empowerment analyses are, they still don't combine for a comprehensive picture of what it takes to *truly* transform a community for the long haul. If you *really* want to help, understand that even with all of those positive steps there are vital pieces still missing from the puzzle.

SOPHIE'S STORY

Sophie is one of my heroes. Anyone who meets her is struck instantly by her joy and her beautiful smile. She radiates peace, joy, and enthusiasm as a business owner, mother, and wife, and it's no wonder that her neighbors in Kiu want to learn the secret of both her financial success and her relentlessly upbeat attitude.

Sophie always had an interest in business, and with three children she knew she needed to supplement her husband's income as a teacher. She even bought a posho mill (a machine used to turn maize into flour) in an effort to bring in some extra money for food and school fees.

But to Sophie's discouragement, that first posho mill enterprise failed. She evaluated the reasons why but had no idea what she did wrong. Then, in 2018, she heard that a Business Start-Up Training

(Yvonne Busolo—410 Bridge)

Sophie and her posho mill.

class was scheduled in her community. She signed up eagerly and almost immediately learned principles that made her rethink her previous approach to business. She learned why her first venture had failed and resolved to turn that failure into future success.

The training started with trusting God, putting Him first in every aspect of the business. Only then did she and her classmates learn about proper and meticulous record-keeping, about taking care of every detail to run their business with excellence, and about putting their customers first. Sophie made a new commitment to generosity, working for the Lord, and running her business with excellence.

Before the thirty-day class had even concluded, Sophie was energized about the possibilities she now saw before her. She bought a second posho mill and threw herself into applying BST principles to its operation. She bought a dairy cow and started selling milk, maize from her farm, and eggs from her family's chickens. She opened a stall in the Kiu public market to sell her goods. She quickly outgrew her small stall and opened a larger, permanent storefront.

Less than three years after completing BST, Sophie was employing between seven and ten people every day on her farm and in her shops. Before she took the training, she employed only one person each day, a growth that proves how powerful the ripple effect from just one well-trained entrepreneur can be in a developing community.

Sophie attributes the brisk growth of her business ventures not only to the new priorities and practices she learned in BST but also to her commitment to giving back. Through BST, Sophie came to understand that glorifying God in business meant giving profits away to help others, and today she sponsors a local orphan—paying her secondary school fees and other school expenses—and mentors young would-be *entrepreneurs in Kiu. "When you get business, you should serve your community," she says. "You don't just keep it for yourself."*

Sophie hopes to continue growing her business operation, renting some of her space in the marketplace to other young businesspeople and expanding the products she sells. As she makes more money, she will employ more people and give more away, making her a powerful force against poverty in her community.

CHAPTER FIVE

While I was head-down building school walls and Erika was interacting with the women and children in Butalale, we realized something separately: despite our good intentions, one of the reasons our "help" was of no moment was because it lacked *depth.* Poverty is a multidimensional problem, and while not all those dimensions are physical, the physical problems are numerous, varied, and in many ways interdependent. We weren't going to truly change anything if we just tackled one or two of those problems—in Butalale's case, a sturdy school building. Besides, a permanent school block, as good as it might be, doesn't guarantee that any of the children will actually leave that school educated. It was the beginning of a realization that led directly to a disciplined new approach: we needed to be a mile deep and an inch wide.

The commitment to this idea was nonnegotiable. We seek to engage in distinct places, usually rural areas, that have a defined sense of community. There's good work being done in different contexts—in orphanages, refugee camps, and urban slums in huge cities like Nairobi and Port-au-Prince—but those efforts require a different approach from that for a rural community. Our goal was long-term, substantive change, which could only be achieved in a place where local people were willing to stay, lead, and invest in their transformation.

Once we vet a community, lay the groundwork with defined outcomes and expectations, and engage local leaders to mobilize and unify their community, attention is drawn to the landscape of physical needs facing the people. It's the opposite of "drive-by" solutions, which is essentially what we did in Butalale and remains an all-too-common and prevalent approach. We (the West) come. We see. We fix. We leave. And in our departure, we may even feel pretty good about ourselves.

Instead of aiming from afar at one particular issue and then moving on, 410 is committed to staying focused on one location for a long period of time, keeping the goal of deeply rooted community transformation at the forefront. While we might support a community as it tackles one issue at a time, we do so with the awareness that every initiative is just one tesserae of a very large mosaic.

IT'S ALL ABOUT RELATIONSHIPS

Depth of engagement—a mile deep and an inch wide—in a place is possible only by building strong relationships. We have to earn the right to be heard, and that happens over time. Building, maintaining, and valuing relationships is at the heart of effective partnership; the degree of intentionality we show in *really* getting to know the people in a community is directly proportional to the depth of that partnership and the long-term impact of the work. Again, as we define it, a true partnership is long term in nature, has a high degree of mutuality, and is rooted in relationships.

Here's a pervasive problem: Too often in the West, we want to *help* the poor without really *knowing* the poor. We don't take the time to truly understand their culture, their struggles, the things that their community strives for and celebrates. We write a check or complete a project and then mentally check a box, but that box makes up a tiny part of the big picture. When we prioritize relationships across the bridge in both directions, the result is genuine change, rooted in trust and accountability.

If our working friendships across the bridge are built on the cornerstone of trust, that stability enhances every conversation, plan, and project that follows. As Bob Lupton says in *Toxic Charity*, "Charity that does not enhance trusting relationships may not be charity at all." If we *really* want to help, our work with the poor must strengthen a trusting relationship that already exists. We don't start with a big, flashy project fueled by our Western idea of a solution, our obsession with progress and efficiency, and a desire for a plaque with our name on it.

The tricky part, once again, is how to *actually* do that. We believe we should limit our efforts to those actions and attitudes that enhance trusting relationships with our partner communities. So, we enter a place only when we've been invited. We do *with,* not *for.* *They* lead, we follow. We allow them to stumble, grow, and fail. And we work at *their* pace, not the donor's.

WHY THINGS GET TOXIC

To fully grasp the nature of genuine, trusting relationships across the bridge, we need to understand the fallout that occurs when relationships originate from the wrong motives. In our own lives, we all recognize what toxic relationships look like. When people we care about persist in relationships that lack reciprocity, mutuality, and accountability, we might intervene out of concern—offering advice whether solicited or not. Our desire is to point out the problem and spare our friend or family member from future pain.

In one sense, interpersonal relationships are different from those with the poor, because when one party starts *helping* the other party, a giver/receiver dynamic is created. The complication increases when the giver starts feeling good about themselves for helping, possibly even feeling superior. But the tricky, potentially toxic dynamics are just as present in those relationships as they are with your friend who keeps falling in love with someone who doesn't carry their weight. Or, similarly, we all understand that we don't help our own children by doing everything for them. For some reason, and I'm not sure why, well-intended people with big hearts and lots of compassion forget the basics of healthy relationships when it comes to helping the poor.

Authentic relationships are reciprocal, accountable, and, yes . . . messy. When one person exclusively gives and the other exclusively receives, especially when the giver's motives are uncertain, what results is not a true relationship at all. Take a connection between a giver and a receiver across the bridge and again put it in the framework of a relationship between a parent and a child. Imagine meeting first-time parents of a newborn child. If you were to ask them what they hope for their child some twenty years into the future when their child will leave their home, I doubt you'd hear, "We hope they have lots of *stuff* when they leave." Of course not. Instead, parents would talk about things like character, faith, integrity, a strong work ethic, and honesty. They would talk about the virtues that will allow their child to thrive long after they leave the comfort and security of their home. But for some reason, when it comes to helping the poor, our actions indicate that we place more importance on *stuff* than we do the virtues that will allow them to thrive long after we are gone.

Connections based solely on needs don't have any of the manifestations of a genuine, mutual relationship; instead, they tend to end abruptly, typically after a short time. And, ironically, despite what the giver thinks of as their pure motives, relationships based on need typically don't even eliminate those needs—they perpetuate them. It's a perplexing scenario that arises again and again when the people writing the checks don't take the time to really *know* the people on the receiving end.

UNINTENDED CONSEQUENCES OF RELATIONSHIPS

Authentic relationships are messy for one obvious reason—people are involved. Relationships are hard enough with the people we know best, so how much more difficult will they be with people we barely know, who may live halfway around the globe in a completely different culture and tradition? We have different upbringings, different priorities, and different ways of looking at the world. All of this makes for a minefield of potential problems and unintended negative consequences.

One of those ugly unintended consequences comes from the potential power imbalance between the giver and the receiver. If you are the giver, you rarely recognize it as a power imbalance. But if you've ever been the receiver, you know it all too well. Power imbalances pop up when relationships become transactional. Said another way, when all we (the givers) focus on is what we give to, or do for, someone, the relationship becomes transactional. The receiver's perceived value of the relationship is dependent on what the giver gives or does.

When one party is always the giver and the other party is always the receiver, the giver risks being seen or perceived as superior to the receiver. This may even be a shared perception— the giver *and* the receiver see the giver as superior. The brutal truth about this perception is that it will rarely be verbalized by either party. The giver would never vocalize a sense of superiority, not because they don't want to risk being seen as arrogant but because, more often than not, they don't even recognize that the dynamic exists. And the receiver would never accuse the giver of being superior because they don't want to jeopardize the gifts they're receiving, even if the receipt of that gift undermines their dignity. While the giver feels a sense of satisfaction, the relationship remains transactional and, consequently, the receiver loses dignity and feels inferior.

One of the ways to prevent this imbalance is to be invited into a relationship by the people we seek to help. When the receiver—the one experiencing need—invites someone into a relationship, they are less likely to see the giver as "them" or "those people" and more likely to seeing the giver as "us." The tricky part is for the giver to continue to subordinate their hoped-for solutions for the receiver to solutions that the receiver thinks are best. After all, we've been invited into *their* reality, not ours. It's like being invited to a party and then barreling in the door and spending the whole evening suggesting ways that the host could make the party better. Not only will you make the party extremely unpleasant but also you will do some serious damage to your relationship with the host.

Another critical element to offsetting a power imbalance and maintaining a positive relationship is participation and mutuality. When both the giver and the receiver participate together in the solution, the receiver no longer sees the solution as someone else's. They take ownership of the solution, and when they contribute with their time, talent, and resources, they maintain and strengthen their dignity. Ideally, the giver will be invited to co-labor on the solution defined by the receiver, which will lead to more sustained results and serve to deepen the relationship.

Ultimately, there must be a caring, ongoing relationship before either one will truly engage in the work. The key is for the individuals on both sides of the bridge to shift their thinking—for the receiver to move from seeing the outsider as a person who is doing something "for" them to seeing the outsider as someone who is "part *of* them" and doing something "with" them. For the giver, the key is to enter humbly, by invitation, to partner and co-labor in the work.

THE TROUBLE WITH POWER

Power struggles are different from power imbalances. Power struggles exist in poor communities and prosperous communities alike—power struggles between interest groups, local leaders, politicians, and neighbors. Each group has its own constituents and its own set of priorities, with a sort of tug-of-war happening all the time. Inject a donor into the mix and it gets even more complicated.

Donors have their own power interests. They have money, an idea, and expectations. Western donors expect things to happen at a certain pace because, once again, in our culture time has authority. They may have a passion for a certain area of need and pay little attention to the priorities that the poor themselves have identified. Donors expect their generosity to be deployed on time and in a certain way, and they may not trust the receiver to use their funds appropriately, so they err on the side of control. They justify it because, after all, they just want to help, and *anything* they do to help the poor must be a good thing, right?

The power interests within the community and the power interests of the donor are often in conflict with each other. The natural question becomes, "Who wins?" Tragically, and all too often, the power interest of the donor prevails. After all, the donor has the money, and thus the receiver, who isn't going to risk damaging the relationship and losing the resources, capitulates.

WHEN GOOD INTENTIONS HIT A DEAD END

Here's a very real example of something I have experienced dozens of times over the years.

Jim and Jackie Jackson met Faith on a medical mission trip to Kenya under memorable circumstances. Faith walked two hours to bring her seven-year-old daughter, who had fallen into the fire in their outdoor wood-burning kitchen, to be treated by an American doctor. Her daughter's burns were severe but treatable. The doctors did what they could and gave Faith some medicine that would last until her daughter's wounds could heal.

Jackie had a chance to chat with Faith, and they became quick friends. She learned that Faith was married and the mother of five children. Her husband traveled to the city every weekday to find work and labored with Faith in their *shamba* (farm) on the weekends. Faith was smart, cheerful, and energetic. Jackie introduced her husband, Jack, to her new friend, and they continued to get to know one another.

During their conversation, the Jacksons learned that two of Faith's four children didn't attend school because of the lack of school fees and a school uniform. Filled with compassion, the Jacksons decided to help. They gave Faith enough money for a school uniform (less than $50). Faith was thrilled and extremely grateful. She shared that somehow, some way, she and her husband would find the resources necessary to cover her children's school fees. They exchanged Facebook information so they could stay in touch. Faith departed, and the Jacksons felt good about what they had done.

Some weeks later, they reconnected on Facebook. When the Jacksons inquired how the children were doing in school, Faith confessed that she and her husband could not find the money to pay for school fees. Everyone knew it would take time, but the next school term was about to begin, and neither the Jacksons nor Faith wanted the children to miss more school, so the Jacksons sent a nominal amount to Faith so all her children could enroll in school.

A few months passed, and a direct message appeared on Jackie's Facebook. One of Faith's children had contracted malaria, and they didn't have money for transportation to see a doctor or for the drugs necessary to treat the disease. No other medical teams were coming to their rural community, and Faith desperately needed Jackie's help. Jackie's desire to help was less enthusiastic than it had been in the previous instances. She hadn't heard from Faith in months, but now that she needed something, here she was again.

The pattern continued for two more years until one day I received a phone call. Jack and Jackie called me to ask for advice. They were fatigued and frustrated, and they needed to find some other way to help Faith. It wasn't my first conversation like this, but I listened patiently. Jackie wanted to know why Faith's situation wasn't improving from the development work we were doing in her community.

I did a little research, and I learned that two of Faith's children were sponsored by another organization and attending school. Her other two children attended school sporadically, but more often than not, they were working as casual laborers in the community to earn money. Faith had been invited to attend our BST but dropped out after the first week, and her husband had declined to join a Foundations for Farming (F4F) training when he was invited. The local leaders in Faith's community were aware of the family's situation, and they told me that Faith would regularly approach visitors for monetary support. They believed she was being helped by multiple families in the US.

That was the last time that the Jacksons helped Faith. The news was heart-wrenching for them. No one wants to be taken advantage of or be misled. No one wants to create dependency or be seen as an easy mark. But when relationships are founded on needs, what starts as a well-intentioned desire to help ends in fractured trust and a serious reluctance to assist someone else in the future. The donor's fatigue hardens their heart. We become suspicious and resentful, and then we disengage. This is not the foundation on which authentic relationships are built.

Maybe you've found yourself in a situation similar to the Jacksons'—moved to action by the needs you witnessed and tempted to help right then and there. After all, the need is right in front of you. You want to help. You're able to help. What, then, should you do to avoid the same fate as the Jacksons? First, don't misunderstand: not everyone is like Faith, and I am certainly not implying that people in need are disingenuous or looking to take advantage of everyone trying to help. The point is that it starts with relationships, not resources or your checkbook.

When visitors to our communities come to us expressing a desire to help someone they've met in the community, the first thing we do is thank them for making us aware of the problem and their desire to help. I am always grateful when people pause, take a breath, and choose to learn how they can *really* help. If Jim and Jackie had started with such a conversation, we could have spoken with the local leaders to determine what, if any, interventions were appropriate. The local leaders would have investigated the situation, if they didn't *already* know, and shared with us an appropriate course of action. In this case, Faith had access to programs that could empower her and her family, but, in her mind, she didn't need to seek long-term empowering assistance. A small portfolio of transactional benefactors was working just fine to her. The relationship could have been built not on repeated requests for money but on encouragement and accountability, as friends on one side of the bridge urge friends on the other side to take advantage of the opportunities before them.

FLIPPING THE SCRIPT

In his book *Toxic Charity*, Bob Lupton describes another troubling aspect of the giver/receiver dynamic that crops up when resources are owned by the outsiders (givers) and the rules are devised by those in control of the resources:

> *The giver-recipient relationship is doomed from the start. Such relationships hardly foster trust. Usually, they breed resentment. The recipient must figure out the rules of the system, determine the kind of appeal most likely to secure the maximum benefit, learn the language that best matches the dispenser's values, and, above all, be sincere. Half-truths are acceptable. Fabrication may be necessary. It doesn't really matter*

because this is about working a system, not joining a community. Givers, then, must continually tighten the rules, close off loopholes, guard against favoritism, and be ever vigilant to detect manipulation or outright fraud. The system lends itself to adversarial relationships.

But instead of lobbying for wholesale change to the paradigm and seeking out ways to make local recipients into insiders who make decisions for their own community, we typically perpetuate a system that seems designed to be gamed by those on the receiving end of it. Lupton offers a solution: "The recipients must become dispensers, authors of the rules, builders of community."

As well as we understand this about our own interpersonal relationships, when it comes to charity, our emotions and adherence to traditional systems tend to trump what we know to be true. The traditional systems perpetuate broken relationships by a dependence on the giver/receiver dynamic. To flip this paradigm, the system itself must change. Recipients need to lead, determine their desired outcomes, actively participate, build their community, and identify and distribute resources.

On the other side of the bridge, the giver's priorities must shift from projects and programs to enhancing trust, restoring dignity, and developing self-sufficiency. Listening to the community, empowering the leaders, and allowing them to lead and be held accountable all foster trust. If we *really* want to help, we must execute with discipline (not emotion) and refuse to compromise the principles of indigenously led, asset-based, participatory development—*development* defined as "what people do for themselves."

A LONG JOURNEY

One of the tenets of traditional poverty alleviation systems is a reliance on results-oriented, cause-and-effect programs—write a check, fix a problem, move on. But when efforts are rooted in real relationships, it's never that simple or tidy. The development process is a long journey. During that journey, a lot must change. But change doesn't happen quickly, and it never happens without setbacks. Results aren't guaranteed—oftentimes unnoticeable in the short run. To *really* help people move out of extreme poverty, lots of things, both physical and nonphysical, need to change. People are changing, and, typically, people don't change easily or quickly. If we *really* want to help, we must have a commitment to walk with them as that change occurs in them and in us.

Because that change doesn't happen quickly, 410 walks alongside our partner communities for a long time. At the core of this walk is our desire to build strong, healthy relationships with people. Not processes. Not projects or programs. Relationships aren't built on the back of development projects. Projects are the fruit of the relationships we build.

The heart of our engagement, as we develop authentic relationships over time, is the process of earning the right to be heard. That means we must listen, not rush the process in the name of results. As Stephen Covey said, "Seek first to understand and then be understood." If our desire is to stand in the gap of what a community cannot do on its own, we must (a) walk alongside them to discern what they *can* do on their own, (b) help them remove the barriers and obstacles for the change *they* want, and (c) patiently encourage and support their efforts to change what they can *on their own*. This requires strong, healthy, trusting relationships.

WHY WE DIVE DEEP

All of this brings us back to the notion of going a mile deep and an inch wide. Depth in our partnerships is vital because if we stay shallow, we fail to see and address the multidimensional needs that keep the people stuck. Not only does a holistic approach touch on the interdependencies that exist between physical areas of need, but also it helps build their capacity for self-development. After all, we are capacity builders—leadership capacity, infrastructure capacity, human capacity, earning capacity, and more.

It's gratifying to see local leaders catch the vision for what can happen in their community and start to understand that they have the capacity to make change a reality. I think of Pastor Boniface in Kwambekenya, Pastor James in Karogoto, and Joseph in Segera, who have been at the heart of their communities' work before we arrived and, then, after the partnership is over, continue to forge ahead to spark change without the need to seek help or validation from outsiders. Empowerment is a muscle that must be used to grow. And the opposite holds true too. The empowerment muscle atrophies when people don't embrace empowerment and look to (or blame) others for the cause of their problems or as the only source of solutions.

When Westerners come in with their money and building supplies and throw all of their energy into a need that they identified without local input and scant attention to fostering relationships, it tends to underscore the indigenous belief that they can't solve their own problems. And since these solutions are done in a piecemeal way, with little regard for follow-up or sustainability, they fail to have a long-term effect on the issues they were designed to address.

Besides local empowerment, another way we measure depth is by the scope of involvement across the entire community. We start with local leaders, but the efforts will be hobbled if those leaders are the *only* ones participating. The goal of any initiative is across-the-board buy-in from every population within a community. I was unsettled when there wasn't a man to be seen around our work site in Butalale, and with good reason: the men are a key group that must engage with community improvement efforts if those initiatives are going to have staying power. When men and women, young and old, farmers and merchants, and people from every corner of the community are engaged in improvement efforts, the results are so evident that neighboring communities take notice.

The role of the outsiders—genuine friends who have been invited in from across the bridge and partnered in the work—is important but leads us to another catalyst for change that takes place in multiple areas of need. The thing that starts the flywheel—something that we can influence to an extent but that really lies with the local people—is the building of capacity across the community.

JACK'S STORY

Jack is a Maasai warrior, a strong man of God, and one of my heroes. As a Maasai, Jack's tribe occupies a societal place in the world that is about as far from modern American culture as you could possibly imagine. Most Maasai people still live according to the traditions that have governed them for hundreds of years; they are seminomadic, following their livestock herds to more fertile lands according to season and rain patterns. Their families are often polygamous, and children are rarely sent to school since the tribe values their herds and learning the ways of their culture more than traditional education.

This was the world that Jack was born into. Jack never knew his father, who died when his mother was seven months pregnant. He was the firstborn male child to his mother and had eight sisters and one younger brother. Jack and his family knew nothing outside the tribal traditions and the preeminent value of cattle and goats to a family's position. But even as the Maasai were battling to maintain their historical practices, the Kenyan government was pressuring Kenyans to enroll children in primary school—at the time, at least one per family. Jack's mother feared the repercussions from the government if she didn't capitulate, so she sent two of Jack's older sisters to school. Jack was to stay back with the herds because he was the treasured firstborn son and his highest calling was to learn to follow in his father's footsteps. In fact, as Jack would explain it, it was common practice to send the "least loved" children to school since it was perceived as sending your child away from the family. This status often fell on the Maasai girls, since they would ultimately marry and leave home anyway. Jack, on the other hand, was seen as the ultimate provider for his family and therefore highly valued.

(Yvonne Busolo—410 Bridge)

(Yvonne Busolo—410 Bridge)

Jack and his wonderful family.

Jack worked long days as a child herding the livestock, until one of several improbable events happened and allowed him to go to primary school. His sisters had dropped out. His eldest sister became pregnant in grade six, and the second sister dropped out during grade three. This was an unexpected and unwelcome surprise for their mother. As punishment for dropping out of school and placing her at risk with the government, Jack's mother gave the girls Jack's responsibilities—herding the goats—and Jack was enrolled in school in their place. She still wasn't convinced that school had any tangible benefit for Jack or the family, but she enrolled him nonetheless in class one—a ten-year-old in a classroom full of kids who were at least four years younger than him.

It was tough going at first because he was significantly older than his classmates and he didn't speak Swahili, which is the language used in Kenyan classrooms. He spoke only his mother tongue of Maa. By class three he had picked up enough Swahili to actually learn, and soon he was showing brisk progress, impressing school administrators who understood the odds he had defied already.

As he sought to concentrate on his studies and still respect the traditions of his people, Jack encountered struggles that weren't common to the average Kenyan child. First, until class four, Jack attended a day school thirteen kilometers from his home. He walked or ran that distance every day. He would leave his home at 5 a.m. and arrive at school at 6:45 a.m. When he rose to grade four and began attending a boarding school, it wasn't unusual for him to come home during term breaks to find that his family had moved to another location to find better grazing lands. He would ask around until he found them, and his mother would find him a Maasai friend to stay with so that he could continue to attend school.

In sixth grade, Jack reached the age when every Maasai young man transitions from a boy to a Maasai warrior—a Moran. It's a fascinating cultural tradition, in which the young men (usually around age fifteen) prove that they have what it takes to care for a family. It starts with a period of isolation. A group of Maasai boys spend a month living alone, wandering the bush, learning Maasai customs, and developing strength, courage, and endurance. They find food at Maasai homes and are typically fed sheep meat, blood, and milk. This period of isolation and wandering culminates with the killing of a lion. Since lions are protected by the Kenyan government, groups of about thirty Maasai boys hunt the lion as a group. When a lion is killed, the entire group is considered to have completed the act.

After they've achieved that feat, they undergo circumcision and then embark on "raids"—traveling long distances to steal cows, goats, and sheep from other villages to prove that they have what it takes to support a household.

Amazingly, despite the many demands of going through the Moran ritual and attending school at the same time, Jack did well on his KCPE, the standardized test given to every eighth grader in the country to determine their next steps. But his mother couldn't spare their precious goats to fund secondary school. His educational journey would have ended there if his mother, by now sold on her only son's potential through the classroom, hadn't raised money within the tribe to send him to a nearby boarding school. This was highly unpopular within her extended family. Jack tells of the time his uncle walked nearly ninety kilometers to rebuke his mother and warn her that if she continued to allow Jack to pursue his education, she would become poor. But send him she did. Jack had the opportunity to matriculate to a high-standard secondary school in Nanyuki, a small city in north-central Kenya, but Jack knew that the cultural transition from the bush to the city would be drastic and difficult, so he opted for a rural secondary school.

After secondary school Jack again figured he had hit a wall; he had, after all, completed more schooling than he could have dreamed of as a young Maasai boy. But he couldn't help but wish for more, especially when the principal at his secondary school encouraged him to pursue either college or, if that was out of reach, a trade school to study accounting. His mother was convinced to sell more goats to enroll him in an accounting course, but during his first year a drought hit the Maasai's territory, the flocks were depleted, and he had to drop out. He started working at a research facility in the area in hopes that he could save enough money to continue his courses. Before he had grown his own nest egg, a college professor met him, identified his potential, and arranged for a university scholarship.

Jack married shortly after secondary school, and when he was preparing for college, he and his wife had a son, Shawn (named after a researcher who befriended Jack). Jack's wife had a very difficult delivery over a four-day period, and Shawn was born with cerebral palsy. Jack describes the first ten years of his son's life as "like a dead person"—unable to walk, sit up, digest food, or talk. They spent years and precious shillings on doctors' visits and physical therapy in hopes that their son would one day be able to walk, run, and play. After medical doctors provided no results, Jack resorted to witch doctors in his village. That, too, was unsuccessful.

By this time, Jack's wife had come to enjoy attending church on Sunday morning. There were precious few churches in the area, and she would walk a long distance every week to attend. Jack was intrigued by what he heard from his wife, but men simply did not attend church with the women and the children. Instead, Jack found a Christian radio broadcast that grabbed his attention. "I liked what this man was saying," he says. "This man's message had something for me." Over time, Jack became more and more committed to biblical teaching, and he ultimately put his faith in Christ.

He and his family started attending Christian "crusades"—three-day revivals—to find healing for their son. They attended ten such crusades over the years without experiencing a healing. On his way to the eleventh crusade, Jack tells the story: "I honestly humbled myself before the Lord and asked that he heal my son. If he did, I would commit my life to his service in whatever way he wanted. I said, 'If my son will get well, I will serve this God. This is where the truth is.' We attended that crusade believing that God was able. After the crusade, we returned home, and the next morning my son woke up very early and was able to walk, sit up, and even talk. It was a miracle."

When I've spoken with Jack about that day in 2010 when he saw a transformation in his son's physical condition, I asked him how he would respond to skeptics in the West. I shared that the typical American, even one who is a devoted Christian, is conditioned not to believe in stories of extraordinary healings. Jack's answer reminds me of the blind man who had to answer doubters after he was healed by Jesus in John 9:25: "I don't know if he is a sinner or not. One thing I know: I was blind but now I see." All Jack knows, all he needs to know, is that he prayed fervently for his son and he experienced a miracle. The boy who could not walk, talk, hold his neck up, or retain food is now a teenager who runs and keeps up with his classmates in school.

Today Shawn is about to finish class eight, sit for his KCPE exam, and go on to secondary school.

After witnessing that miracle, Jack started looking for opportunities to give himself to God's work out of gratitude for what the Lord had done for his family. The fulfillment of that quest came two years after his son's healing, when Jack was returning home from his weeklong work at the research facility. He decided to visit a friend before returning to his home. His friend told him a faith-based organization called 410 Bridge was interviewing for a staff position in the area. Jack knew nothing about 410 Bridge, but as he learned more and more, he knew that job was meant to be his. After the interview he was going to head back home, but when someone told him that he might not have sufficient cell service to receive the follow-up call from the interview, he stayed put. He wasn't going to do anything to jeopardize the opportunity he felt God had placed in front of him.

The odds were against Jack being chosen for the job; there were seventeen other applicants, many of whom had more background and more connections with 410 Bridge. As Jack tells it, "I knew that job was mine. I just knew it." And it was. Today Jack serves his fellow Maasai and the other tribes in his community, teaching them to trust and follow the Lord and giving them the tools to succeed and serve their neighbors.

Jack stands as a striking example of the way God can carve a new life's road for one of his followers to help fulfill his greater plan. Jack is one of my heroes. His son's healing is undoubtedly a miracle, but as he tells his story, he sees that his road has been marked with one miracle after another—a series of doors opened by the Lord giving him new opportunities to serve and glorify him. Thank you, Jack, for all you do.

CHAPTER SIX

The old adage about teaching a man to fish feels too overstated to be useful these days, but it remains a powerful, if oversimplified, nod to the need to create more capacity among the members of a poor community. The nature of a true partnership is that it is mutual, empowering, and long term. But in the context of a partnership with a community, "long term" doesn't mean permanent. If we didn't make building capacity a priority over the life of a partnership, it would be very difficult to ever work ourselves out of a job. But if we place the development of long-term, locally sourced empowerment at the core, we see how our involvement lights a spark for a flame that keeps burning by the people who need the warmth the most. If we *really* want to help, we can help them keep that fire lit by building capacity.

WE ARE CAPACITY BUILDERS

The amount of research, studies, and opinions on the issue of capacity creation could fill a large room. And rightly so. It's a complex topic, and while we can learn plenty from all the experts, our approach is more of a pragmatic, "boots-on-the-ground" perspective—what empowerment is and how it can be achieved in real, everyday practice. In our experience, we see a tremendous lift by distilling the complexity down to two areas: infrastructure capacity and people capacity.

In most of our communities, the LCs initially identify infrastructure problems that keep them and their neighbors from thriving. These are the problems that are immediately evident to anyone visiting the community—issues like access to safe water, crumbling school buildings, electricity, small or nonexistent health facilities, and subpar roads. It's exceedingly difficult to instill capacity in people when they struggle to meet their daily needs because of glaring infrastructure constraints, which is why those barriers are prioritized early in the partnership. But infrastructure initiatives are expensive in both time and money. In many cases, community-wide infrastructure projects take years to complete.

In a perfect world where resources and solutions align, completing all the infrastructure projects and then moving to the people-oriented programs might make sense, but that's not how it works. If it did, communities would be waiting years for water and education infrastructure to be completed before the people capacity programs begin. This may leave them feeling frustrated by the lack of progress. The reality is that with a holistic approach that is a mile deep and an inch wide, multiple things can happen in a community at one time, provided the community can *absorb* and *participate* in a healthy way. Some people capacity programs—entrepreneurship trainings, education programs, etc.—occur while we are planning and working through the infrastructure initiatives. The gains are modest because not everyone has the physical capacity to be trained in business or farming or to attend school. But we do it anyway. Then, as the community makes headway on infrastructure capacity, the gains are multiplied through the people capacity programs, both in adoption of the trainings and in the impact that's made.

Karima is a great example. Access to safe water in closer proximity to homesteads was a fundamental part of Karima's development. A centrally located borehole with several large distribution tanks throughout the community took years to complete. One of those tanks was to be constructed at Kawamaitha Primary, but because of its location, the connection was one of the last construction phases. To wait for the water to be completed before helping the school improve the quality of education was a nonstarter for the leaders, though they knew that without safe water at the school, students would not perform to their potential.

Quality improvement initiatives ran concurrently with the long process of bringing safe water to the community. The improvement in the school was palpable but, again, not to the level that it could have been. The community felt the difference, nonetheless. They saw positive change. Test scores rose modestly, which fueled more involvement from the community. By the time the water line reached the school, the community did more to complete that project on their own than during any prior phase.

UNDERSTANDING THE PARTS OF THE WHOLE

We place a premium on instituting a holistic, comprehensive approach to capacity building while still focusing on individual areas of need within each community. I use the word "holistic," but I don't mean shaving your head, growing a long beard, and burning incense. It's simply that the approach is comprehensive, seeking to address every major area of development so that one issue isn't addressed to the exclusion or dismissal of others. The 410 Bridge model is predicated on four major physical areas of development that, if addressed with discipline and local owner-ship, can transform a community by building its capacity to solve its own problems: water, education, economic empowerment, and health/wellness.

One of the most striking, if not obvious, realities is how inextricably linked these four areas are. None of the priorities can stand alone when considered in light of a community's long-term goals. If we *really* want to help, it would be completely counter to our philosophy to come into a community and just do a water project, or just build a school block, or just train farm-ers and entrepreneurs. Our efforts will hit a dead end unless we capitalize on the interlocking nature of a community's various needs. I often call them interdependencies, which speaks to the idea that by addressing one need, we move closer to the prog-ress of another. But it's more than interdependence. We've seen firsthand the multiplicative effect when you address all of the needs together, over time, in a place. You can't move the needle in one area without advancing one or more of the others.

The lack of safe, accessible water impacts the capacity of women and children, so when you solve a water problem, you also eliminate an education barrier and an economic development barrier. Safe water also impacts health. When you remove the unsafe water problem, you dramatically improve health and wellness. It's obvious to most that education will positively impact economic development, but less obvious is the impact education has on health and wellness. And without broad economic development, the community will never be able to sustain their water, education, and other social programs. If we *really* want to help, we have to dive deep, in multiple areas, over time and leverage the interdependent benefits of a comprehensive approach.

WHY WATER IS KEY

In most cases, when we enter a community, we learn that residents lack access to clean water. Anyone with even a casual understanding of the developing world understands the endemic nature of the safe water problem. There's a good reason why it's usually the first priority for LCs. The simple reality is that many of the desired outcomes, like economic empowerment and quality education, can't even be realized until the water issue is addressed. When we are invited into a community, we usually learn that residents (commonly women and children) are walking very long distances to polluted water sources—rivers, water pools, or shallow wells—to get water for their family, and more often than not, they make that trip multiple times each day.

This simple act of gathering the family's daily water takes hours and strips women and children of the capacity to do other productive things. The women don't have the capacity to start a small business or care for their households. The children are late to school and don't have time for homework. Children can't focus on academics, which limits their ability to advance beyond primary school, thus triggering the negative consequences that a lack of a quality education brings. Even if they were able to qualify for secondary school, their parents may not have the income for school fees, often because the mother doesn't have the capacity to start a small business or produce an income.

And that's not to mention the devastating health effects that unsafe water has on the community. Waterborne diseases—especially harmful to young children—create another capacity obstacle for children to attend school or to work to advance themselves. In short, the pursuit of water can be all consuming, and until that barrier is eliminated, it's all but impossible for local leaders to build the capacity for further development.

There have been instances when a LC decides not to prioritize access to water. In some communities, the local leaders go through their assessments and determine that their water is "safe enough" or "accessible enough," so they prioritize another development area. This is partially driven by their experience that Western supporters are project driven and not long term oriented. They know that the well-wishers come to do a project, then leave. As a result, when leaders define their water situation as "good enough," they prioritize another project so as not to miss out on the support from their new project-centric friends. But over time, most communities will revisit the water issue, because the current situation constrains capacity and remains a barrier to their development.

WATER IS MORE THAN LIFE

Water is life. It's a statement that we hear all the time, and it couldn't be truer. Without water, communities can't develop. But water is also power—political power. Those who control access to water, or even the promise of access to water in the future, gain power and control. Election-season promises for water systems are favorites on the campaign trail. And those who "serve" on water councils control people's access to water and the revenue that it generates. These are two realities that manifest into empty promises and possible corruption.

A classic example occurred in Karogoto, Kenya, a community just east of the Aberdare Mountains. When we first arrived in Karogoto, the people drew their water from a small, polluted, but fast-moving stream that ran through their community. To get to the stream, women and children would traverse very narrow paths alongside a steep and slippery hill. I personally made the journey several times and never once kept my footing. How they navigated it carrying a twenty-liter (forty-five-pound) jerry can strapped to their back remains a mystery to me.

Karogoto is downstream from a coffee-processing facility where coffee beans are washed, dried, and processed. During harvest season, the water smells and tastes like weak, stale coffee.

Our first water project was to move the water, by way of a self-powered ram pump, about four hundred meters uphill to a newly constructed small storage tank in the center of the community. Even though the water was unfiltered, the community saved time and peril by not having to navigate the treacherous hillside to retrieve water. But as helpful as it was, the solution was insufficient. The tank was small, the water remained unsafe, and it did not serve the entire community.

About a year later, it was brought to our attention that a huge (500,000-liter) water holding tank sat just outside the center of the community. In fact, it was less than 150 meters from the small tank that was just constructed. The tank was massive. It was built fifteen years prior to our arrival, but we never saw it because it was hidden by a decade of plant growth. The tank had never held one drop of water. Politicians made promises of water but never followed through. When we asked the leaders why they never mentioned the holding tank, they said that it didn't belong to them. It wasn't viewed as an asset by the community. They saw it as a monument to a previously elected official and not something they could leverage for their own. Stories like this one are common, as people in power seize on the need for water and use it to curry favor or win votes without ever really solving the water problem.

After some discussion, the leaders became advocates for their community and easily got permission from the government to use the tank. Today, that tank has been refurbished, and it is the central distribution hub for multiple distribution tanks around Karogoto. Clean water is supplied by a deep-water borehole that provides safe water to the entire community.

SEEKING REAL WATER SOLUTIONS

Over the years we've concluded that many of the water "solutions" aren't really solutions at all, whether power-hungry politicians are involved or not. Sometimes families with means will dig shallow wells on their property for their own use, keeping them from public use with guards, walls, or fences. But the private wells are shallow and prone to dry up when there's no rain. Even when they do yield water, they aren't deep enough to produce safe water. In addition to private wells, the landscape is littered with shallow public wells operated with hand pumps—the water solution of choice for several prominent water-focused organizations. They are relatively cheap and simple to install, but even though they seem to be everywhere, hand-pump wells are an imperfect fix.

A widespread study of water resources and access in Malawi and Zambia underscores my belief that hand pumps are not an effective long-term fix for a community seeking safe and consistent water availability that can support development. The study, conducted by the Scottish University of Strathclyde in partnership with various NGOs and government partners, found that only 58 percent of the water points that had been improved by outside organizations were actually functional. Further research by the Rural Water Supply Network echoes Strathclyde's findings; the RWSN report found that 36 percent of the hand pumps installed were no longer operating, and a follow-up stated that 15 percent of the water points were nonfunctional after just one year, and 25 percent weren't working after four years.

Solving the water problem starts with access. For every water project where water isn't available aboveground (rivers, streams, springs), we must look belowground. The first step is to dig a hole, but the depth of that hole makes a significant difference in the quality of the water. Many of the organizations that dig hand-pump wells typically go only 100 to 150 feet, which may not be deep enough to avoid contamination. Once the well is dug, residents get water by operating the hand pump and filling jerry cans. Or at least that's the way it's supposed to work. The sad reality is often different; the hand pump ultimately breaks, and beneficiaries rarely have the parts or the training to repair it on their own. After it breaks, it is either locked or sits idle until the organization that installed it comes to fix it. So, it's back to the river, or wherever community members have always walked for hours a day for unsafe water.

The chief issue with "drive-by" water projects like shallow wells comes back to capacity building. We've seen all too often that when well-intentioned organizations come into a community and put in a shallow well, the residents don't have ownership of the project or the capacity to maintain it. They may not spend any of their time or resources to install it, and the water is free. They view it as a charitable intervention from outsiders, and they rarely have the parts, the expertise, or the money to take care of repairs when the pump breaks down. And like any machine, the pump *will* require repair. Since outsiders presented the solution and came into their community to install it, they'll wait for the same outside agencies to return and fix it when something goes wrong.

This is not to say that all hand-pump solutions are inappropriate. In extremely remote areas, where large-scale water systems are simply not possible, a hand pump may be the only option. The problem, from my perspective, is that the landscape seems to be littered with inoperable shallow-well hand pumps, irrespective of the location. And for us, we're not trying to solve a water problem—we're trying to solve a poverty problem, and a hand-pump solution is nothing more than an ineffective Band-Aid in a community-wide development context.

The same holds true for individual water filters. Providing a water filter to a household will reduce the waterborne diseases and improve their health, but water filters do not increase people's capacity because they still must walk long distances to the water source. And filters are rarely indigenously sustainable, and therefore, they are short-term answers. If people do not have the economic capacity to replace the filter over time, the program fades away. I've had many water filter organizations present their solutions to us in hopes that we would consider distributing their filters to 410 communities. But, once again, we're not trying to solve a water problem. We're trying to solve a poverty problem, and water filters will not get us there. In the very rare instances where we have distributed household water filters, we've done so as a temporary stop-gap measure to improve the health of the community as we embark on a large infrastructure water solution.

Given that focus, our approach to the water problem is completely different. When local leaders pinpoint water as a top priority, we walk them through a process that is more expensive and more involved than water filters or a few shallow wells with hand pumps scattered around their community. Our water process is worth the effort and the cost, because it creates a solid, transformative foundation on which the other aspects of holistic community development efforts can stand.

One of our largest church partners experienced firsthand the shortcomings of the shallow well and hand-pump method. Their attempt to bring safe water vis-à-vis dozens and dozens of hand pumps to sub-Saharan Africa was anything but successful. Pumps were quickly in disrepair, and people were left no better off than before they started the effort. Thankfully, though, this didn't temper their passion to bring safe water to the people who needed it the most. They committed to a multiyear grant to help 410 Bridge communities construct fifty large-scale water solutions that impact nearly 200,000 people. Today those projects are all being operated and indigenously sustained by the local communities. Moreover, those water solutions provide a tangible capacity-building lift to the communities they serve.

WHEN ARE WE FINISHED WITH WATER?

Early in the LC planning process, we ask the leaders what *outcome* they seek from a water solution. Too often, organizations come in with a prefab solution without considering the desired outcome. That desired outcome, in a holistic context, is more than just access to safe water. Leaders will say something like, "Our water outcome will be reached when 80 percent of our households have access to clean, safe water within a ten-minute walk of their homes." From there, we can take stock of the physical features of that community to determine the most effective and affordable way to help them reach their outcome. If the community has a river running through it, we may help the LC plan and install a system that pumps the water from the river, purifies it, and collects it in an elevated tank for distribution elsewhere.

If there's no aboveground water, we have to locate underground water, which requires hydrogeological surveys and then, when the right area is located, the hiring of contractors to drill a borehole and install a solar-powered pump and multiple distribution tanks around the community. Whereas the shallow wells are typically dug to a maximum of 150 feet, the standard for a borehole in Kenya is typically four-hundred-plus feet, which ensures clean and abundant water. Residents participate by donating land, digging trenches, and laying pipe so that the water pumped from the borehole can be distributed to multiple access points throughout the community. When families participate in providing clean, plentiful water out of a spigot in their compound or at a distribution point just down the road, the effect on their day-to-day life is truly transformational, and they have the newfound capacity to do other things.

To guarantee the sustainability of water projects, we recommend that the LC create a water subcommittee. The subcommittee is made up of one or two LC members, but the majority of subcommittee members come from outside the LC, which increases community involvement and exposure to leadership. The water subcommittee is tasked with establishing the fee system so that residents have a stake in their water supply and a fund to draw from when repairs become inevitably necessary.

Some communities have water meters in their compounds, while others have kiosks at nearby distribution points for the collection of the fees. In every case, those who use the water are required to invest in the system's ongoing maintenance.

It can't be overstated how important it is that the fee structure be established *before* water starts flowing. A major lesson learned is that if people start accessing water for free, it is very difficult to get them to pay for water in the future. The local leaders have to remind their neighbors of previous water efforts, where the water was free but things didn't work out. They emphasize the fact that building a stronger community requires everyone to take ownership and responsibility of every solution, especially water. There is a formal document that establishes the roles and responsibilities of the subcommittee and the residents. It's far from perfect, and a litany of issues need to be addressed throughout the process, necessitating an abundance of communication with the community. Importantly, that communication needs to come from the leaders, not outsiders. It's their community. It's their water project. And it's their responsibility.

Karima is, once again, just one example of a community that has been renewed by an efficient water program designed to serve everyone. Our partnership in Karima concluded years ago, but the local water committee is still doing its job—monitoring each part of the system, collecting fees, and arranging for repairs when they become necessary. The history of our involvement in Karima definitively begins with water; after water became safe and available, the people there had the freedom to focus more attention on education for their children and economic development for themselves. When I visited Karima recently, my friend Simon, a former LC member and the monitor of one of the community's water tanks, stopped our group and insisted that we take a moment to enjoy a cup of cool, clean water that he proudly served us from his backyard spigot. Karima's water system has been indigenously sustainable for over ten years, and we couldn't be prouder of their efforts.

HEALTH: THE RIGHT INTERVENTIONS AND OUTCOMES

The need for safe and available water is straightforward and easy to understand, even if the methods to achieve that goal can vary broadly. But when it comes to health, the situation is more complicated than it seems. No one in the community development world would deny the need for better health outcomes for people living in poverty, but too often those of us on the Western side of the bridge misunderstand what the promotion of healthy living in poor rural communities really looks like.

Community health is undeniably important. In 2015 three of the UN's eight Millennium Development Goals were health related: reduce child mortality, improve maternal health, and combat HIV/AIDS, malaria, and other diseases. According to the WHO's Poverty and Health study:

> *They* [*the poor*] *have higher than average child and maternal mortality, higher levels of disease, and more limited access to health care and social protection. And gender inequality disadvantages further the health*

of poor women and girls. For poor people especially, health is also a crucially important economic asset. Their livelihoods depend on it. When poor people become ill or injured, the entire household can become trapped in a downward spiral of lost income and high healthcare costs . . . Good health contributes to development in a number of ways: it increases labor productivity, educational attainment and investment, and it facilitates the demographic transition.

Health is inherently valuable to all individuals, and a healthy community is a central tenet to the reduction of poverty. The tricky part is to determine the strategic interventions that would provide the greatest lift to the overall health and wellness of the community and to identify the outcomes we should actually seek as we help partner communities pursue better health as it relates to the poverty problem.

Because of our own nation's complicated battle for health-care availability, we are quick to focus on *access* to health care rather than helping people become healthier. Said another way, health and wellness do not necessarily mean health care. When it comes to rural extreme-poverty environments, well-wishers tend to assume that we can improve community health if we just build health clinics in places that lack them. In fact, that's the first big project 410 Bridge undertook with the local leaders in Kwambekenya, our first community. But even though that clinic is still operating today and seeing hundreds of patients a month, we view the construction of clinics differently now. Too often, a health clinic is limited by broken government promises related to staffing or resources, and sometimes the issues that hinder local people from getting to health-care facilities can be solved in a less expensive way than erecting a clinic.

In the beginning, we were confused. We brought our Western perspective to the health discussion. We conflated the pursuit of a healthy community with health care. Looking back on it, I can see how the US narrative on access to affordable health care reinforced what we heard from our first few communities. Like us, they saw the issue as an access problem. We must survey the health situation through a big-picture lens, understanding that the most significant gains in community health can often be achieved through seemingly small interventions.

One program that 410 has undertaken in Kenya involves training local volunteers to educate their neighbors on health measures like storing water indoors so that disease-carrying mosquitoes don't breed, teaching proper handwashing to deter disease, and promoting basic household sanitation practices. By equipping these community health advocates, the word gets out about simple habits that can make a big difference in preventing illness.

Additionally, the most effective community health measures are inextricably linked to other key development areas. When you improve the quality and accessibility of water, the incidence of waterborne disease goes way down. When you incorporate public health education into public school curricula, children educate their parents and healthier habits prevail. When you train entrepreneurs and farmers and spur economic development, families can afford better water storage, healthier households, public transportation to clinics, medicine, and preventive measures.

We want our communities to be as healthy as possible; without good health the residents of our partner communities wouldn't have the capacity to improve their lives. But running health programs from a Western perspective, with a focus on access and buildings, isn't our thing. We see it differently now, realizing that other investments—in water, education, economic development, and advocacy—provide a big lift.

QUALITY EDUCATION FOR ALL

It's amazing to see a community start to realize its potential when water access is no longer a constant concern. Once water access has been addressed, LCs frequently turn their attention to education. The local leaders nearly always know that the schools in their community aren't what they could be. When we start a new partnership, we share with the LC our tentpole for education: that 100 percent of the children in their community have access to a quality education at least through the end of primary school (eighth grade in Kenya).

That goal can seem unattainable at the beginning because the barriers to a quality education are numerous and varied. It's not unusual to find a rural community in which a large percentage of the kids don't even attend primary school because their parents don't value education. Maybe the parents are farmers or herders, and they know that their children are going to follow in their footsteps, so they think school is unnecessary. Maybe they live in one of the more remote communities in which families still give their daughters away in arranged marriages at a very young age, so school isn't a priority for those girls. Those attitudes are some of the barriers to lifting a community's educational opportunities— but there are so many more.

When we took our initial tours of the schools in communities like Kwambekenya and Karogoto, we were struck by the same type of conditions that sent me to Butalale in 2005. If the classroom buildings were constructed of bricks or quarry rock, they were extremely rundown, and many were makeshift wooden structures with dirt floors. Most schools didn't have water access or feeding programs, deficiencies that made it hard for students to stay in school or learn effectively. Often, families lacked sufficient food to send lunch with their children, so when lunchtime arrived, the kids would either leave in hopes of finding something to eat or stay and be so hungry that they struggled to concentrate.

Textbooks were so scarce that five or six students shared one tattered book, making homework or studying outside of school hours impossible. Schools would rarely have enough teachers; the government might supply five or six teachers for a school with eight classes, so the school had to combine grade levels, hire a parent as an unqualified teacher, or ask students to teach themselves. And teachers didn't have necessary supplies, like practice tests for the all-important standardized exams given at the end of each school year. Some parents lacked the school fees or money for the required uniforms, so they felt they had no choice but to keep their children at home. Technically, the primary schools that serve our communities in Kenya are public schools, and free primary school education is mandated, but because the government doesn't provide enough teachers or supplies, the school's PTA also requires a contribution from each family. If families don't pay their school fees, their children may be sent home.

In one of our partner communities in Haiti, a primary school didn't exist at all. Over 80 percent of the children weren't going to school because they didn't have the money or means to get there. The need for a local primary school was as obvious as it was heartbreaking, and the leaders asked us to help them construct a school. The emotional response would have been "Sure!" and off we would go with construction. But it's not that simple. If we *really* wanted to help, we needed to be certain that the community could sustain a primary school long into the future. We wanted to make sure that they had the capacity and commitment to maintain the school before we laid a single brick.

We challenged them to show us they could start and operate a school without us. We asked them to start with what they had. It's a painful—borderline heartless—request in many Westerners' eyes. The perception that they had nothing, and therefore couldn't possibly start a school, was a fair criticism. Besides, if they could start a school without us, why hadn't they already done so? But that question is rooted in our Western perspective. Helping them build a school that they could never sustain wasn't going to help anyone, and the leaders knew it.

The community rose to the occasion. They put up poles and tarps to serve as temporary classrooms, constructed benches for the kids to sit on, and hired teachers with contributions from parents. They took the initiative in collecting school fees and buying what was necessary to get their new makeshift school off the ground, and before long 410 Bridge—convinced that this community was motivated to help themselves—assisted them in building a permanent school building. Today, that school is sustained by the community, and 100 percent of the students qualify for secondary school.

A NEW KIND OF SPONSORSHIP

Since our firm goal is always to elevate education for *every* student in a community, we knew we had to sidestep the traditional 1:1 child sponsorship program run by many other organizations. We weren't interested in helping only "the sponsored few" to the exclusion of the other kids in a community, but we also saw the upside of connecting a sponsor relationally with an individual child. Besides, what better way to stay connected to a community than to walk alongside a child on their journey of development? Our solution was to offer student sponsorships in our partner communities but to frame them in a completely different way.

Our sponsorship program connects a sponsor to a specific child whom they can write to and even visit, and if direct needs are identified in that child's life, we may step in to help. But the money given by a sponsor helps more than the individual sponsored child; it lifts the quality of education for that child's *entire* primary school. Every single child who attends that school benefits. We typically don't need to sponsor every student in a school to improve the quality of education for all the students. In Kenya, if we can sponsor one-third of the student population, that money can be used to hire new teachers, buy textbooks and other supplies, improve the infrastructure, start a feeding program, and institute other necessary improvements so that *every* child can access a quality education.

A HIGHER REGARD FOR EDUCATION

Before we could help LC members plan for significant educational improvements, we needed to understand the dynamics of the school system and the specific barriers that keep children from advancing. Country matters. Culture matters. Community dynamics matter. That's another reason why our indigenous staff is so important. We will never truly understand how to *really* help with education if we simply apply our flawed American educational perspective to their system.

The most important event in the life of a Kenyan child is the standardized test known as the KCPE (Kenya Certificate of Public Education), which is given to every child at the end of class eight. Their score on that test decides whether they will attend secondary school at all. If they perform well enough, their score dictates the quality level of their secondary school. The higher their score, the better their secondary school. It carries a ton of weight, and families place a great deal of importance on how their child does on the KCPE.

Students who score more than 400 out of the maximum 500 points (about 5 percent of students) are assigned to the top-tier secondary school (National Schools). Those who score between 300 and 400 (about 25 percent) qualify for the second-tier schools (Extra County Schools), and those who score between 200 and 300 qualify for the third-tier schools (County Schools). Children who don't make at least a 200 have some options (sub-County), but they are limited, and, for all intents and purposes, they are finished with their education. In most cases, when we started working in Kenyan communities, very few students ever qualified for National or Extra County schools.

Through infrastructure projects and quality improvement programs funded by our unique child sponsorship program, we've seen a profound change in the way parents and students view education. After only a few years, 25 to 75 percent of the students in some of our schools were qualifying for National and Extra County schools, and many younger kids who had never considered attending school past the eighth grade were putting their heads down and studying so that they could further their educations. It was a great success story, but it brought its own financial challenge because of the prohibitive cost of secondary school.

The best secondary schools are typically boarding schools and are expensive. Parents pay most of the cost for their children to attend secondary school. We couldn't create a situation where students worked hard to qualify for secondary school but were forced to stay home because their families couldn't afford the school fees. So, we added an additional sponsorship opportunity, promising our partner communities that the top scorers on the KCPE each year could earn a scholarship to secondary school. Qualifying for the program was based on need but didn't absolve the parents from helping pay for some school expenses. It has been incredibly gratifying to talk with young people who completed secondary school curricula and, in many cases, college or university, as they describe their future career plans. These are students who would have likely been forced to stop at eighth grade, either because of educational or financial limitations or because their parents didn't see the value in education beyond primary school.

Water and education are typically the first and second priorities for most LCs, so we spend much of the early part of our partnerships gaining ground in each area. But holistic community development doesn't stop there. From the bedrock foundation of ensuring clean water for all to eliminating the barriers to a quality education for 100 percent of children, we create strong momentum to build even more capacity in our communities.

When we started, I had a pretty strong opinion that education was the backbone of development. I was wrong.

CRISPOH'S STORY

Of the hundreds, if not thousands, of people I've met since my time at 410 Bridge, certain people stand out as special. Crispoh is one of those people and is one of my heroes.

Crispoh's life to this point can be defined by two powerful forces: deep, trusting relationships and faithful service to his community. His investment in the former has helped provide him an incredible range of opportunities to fulfill his calling to the latter.

He is a native of the bush country in the Laikipia region of Kenya we know as Segera. The drive to Segera from Nanyuki, the nearest city, is nearly an hour of dry, dusty roads studded with potholes. As a vehicle approaches, shrouded in dust, its driver is forced on a slalom course of sorts, weaving back and forth to avoid the craters. Located essentially on top of the equator, Segera is so dry that in a period of

(Anna Dower—410 Bridge)

drought, that same drive will take you past dead animals on the side of the road. I remember seeing a woman carrying a zebra's head along that road once; the zebra had died of dehydration because the land was so severely parched. Even in the best of times Segera is a difficult, unforgiving place to live and farm.

Crispoh originally attended a primary school in an old stable until his father, looking to provide his son with a better educational opportunity, sent him to a boarding school with more resources much farther away. But when his father got sick and died during his teen years, Crispoh was compelled to drop out of school to help care for his mother and sisters.

Without a higher education, he was likely destined for a life much like those of his father and grandfather: farming unproductive, semiarid land and tending livestock. But instead, he stumbled on an opportunity to work for an American researcher at the Segera Ranch, a 25,000-acre conservation and research facility near his community. He worked hard as a driver, local guide, and whatever else was asked of him. Soon he was entrusted with a range of responsibilities like helping with primate research projects and driving the researchers around the massive property.

When Carlton "Pappy" Gleason moved to Segera in the early 2000s after his daughter and her husband acquired the Segera Ranch, he and Crispoh became fast friends. Pappy was an amazing man of God and another one of my heroes, though I knew him only briefly. After retiring from his second career, Pappy, at the age of eighty-six, moved to the Segera area. He planted a church and a mission facility just outside the ranch, becoming a missionary to the people of Segera. He was filled with incredible vision and energy, growing the mission to include a small primary school, health clinic, and training facility. I had come to know Pappy for the eighteen months prior to his death, and I would say that getting to know him was one of the greatest honors of my life. He was a truly unique and incredible man, with an amazing legacy.

Pappy became a mentor to Crispoh. Crispoh would tell you that Pappy was more than a mentor and loved him like a son. He started as a driver, and over time Pappy gave him more and more responsibility at the Segera Mission, ultimately entrusting him with management of the operations. Pappy's trust in Crispoh, and his living example of dreaming big dreams for the kingdom of God, had a tremendous impact on the younger man, culminating in the day when Pappy told Crispoh that he believed God was calling Crispoh to be the chaplain at Segera Mission. After praying about it, Crispoh agreed and became a pastor to the people served by the mission. But that calling was threatened in 2008 when Pappy died and the leadership of the Segera Mission changed.

Soon Crispoh was unexpectedly entangled in family drama from Pappy's heirs that overflowed to local politics. There was a power vacuum in the area, filled with new outsiders who knew little about the dynamics of the communities or culture. Vicious rumors were being spread throughout the community about Crispoh, essentially forcing him out of his Segera Mission role. On top of everything else, with his job gone and his reputation hanging in the balance, Crispoh's young daughter became very ill. She was diagnosed with a brain tumor and was not expected to survive.

I met Crispoh shortly before Pappy died in 2008, when we were invited to establish a partnership with the communities served by the mission. As I got to know Crispoh, I found him to be an impressive young man, and I was confused about the stories that were being told about him. I trusted Pappy's judgment and knew that he had truly loved and trusted Crispoh. On the other hand, I was not a fan of the new leadership at the mission, their character, and their tactics. Like Crispoh, we, too, experienced wild accusations about our motives, our character, and our commitment to Christ. When Crispoh was dismissed from the mission, I immediately approached him to join 410 Bridge as the community coordinator for our two communities in the Segera area (Endana and Ereri), a decision I have never come to regret.

I remember walking alone with him that day and asking, "Crispoh, it's just you, me, and God here, and I want to know, are these accusations true?" He replied, "Kurt, as God as my witness, they are not true." His countenance, his humility, and his word were enough for me. That statement, plus what I already knew of his character, was all I needed to hear. We hired him to coordinate our fledgling work in that sprawling Segera area, where he walked (and later motorbiked) countless miles every week to invest in the Gospel-centered, self-developing capabilities of his neighbors.

Crispoh has a vibrant, widespread impact today because of his faith and his integrity, even in the face of tremendous opposition. Relatively quickly, and not unexpectedly, the dysfunctional leadership at the mission turned over and Crispoh's reputation in his community was restored. He is a humble servant to his people, and he is thriving. Against all odds, his daughter's brain tumor was treated and, by all accounts, healed. Today she is attending secondary school.

Despite all the hardships, Crispoh prioritized relationships—with the people in his community, his family, Pappy, me, and 410 leadership. His trust in God never wavered, and he knew that God would open doors if he sought to follow him daily, no matter what. His work in the community he loves is ongoing, but his legacy will be one of faithfulness and multiplication, as younger generations see his impact and resolve to invest in their community like he has.

And as for the fruit of his work? Today, like so many 410 communities, Endana and Ereri have community-wide access to safe, indigenously sustainable water systems, a thriving new business center, high-performing primary schools, and the first-ever university graduates. Endana and Ereri have since graduated from their partnerships with 410, but Crispoh's work continues in a neighboring community, and he now oversees the Hope Savings Group program.

CHAPTER SEVEN

Prevailing wisdom about elevating the quality of life within developing communities goes like this: it all starts with education. I used to think that was true, but now I think the linchpin isn't education. It's economic development.

Don't get me wrong. Education is a critical component to break the cycle of extreme poverty, but there are a couple of realities that led me to change my thinking that economic improvement is the backbone of development. One reality is that one of the primary barriers for children to access a quality education can be eliminated by raising household incomes. A family's inability to afford school fees or a school uniform is often the primary reason a child doesn't attend school. Granted, attendance doesn't necessarily ensure a quality education, but it starts with a child's participation in school. If the parents can't afford to send their child to school, all the quality improvement in the world won't make a difference.

The other important issue is sustainability. Kids are dependent. Even if we're successful in lifting the quality of education in a school, those quality-improvement initiatives can't be sustained without adequate resources within the community. So, the key to improving education, and sustaining that improvement over time, is putting more money into the community, otherwise known as economic development. But how best to achieve that goal?

Those who trumpet education as the starting point would say that the people obviously need jobs, so by lifting the quality of education, the future workforce will be better equipped to go out and find those jobs. I'm not arguing against educating future workers, and no one would argue that people finding jobs is a good thing, but it's more complex than that.

In rural poor communities overseas, the type of jobs you might think of when you search for employment in the US are virtually nonexistent. There are no big companies employing large numbers of people and very few retail establishments outside of the mom-and-pop variety. For Kenyans to find jobs, they would need to move to urban centers like Nairobi, where finding a good-paying job is more of a myth than a reality. One of the reasons for the propagation of the urban slums in Nairobi is the fact that people flock from rural Kenya to Nairobi in search of a better standard of living—jobs, better education for their children, etc. Unfortunately, that's not the reality. A 2014 study from the African Population and Health Research Center found that about 2.5 million people, or 60 percent of Nairobi's population, live in slums in the capital city, and about 50 percent of those slum dwellers are unemployed.

MAKING EMPLOYERS, NOT EMPLOYEES

That's why we prefer developing employers over employees. A better-educated potential employee, unable to find work, does little to move the needle in our communities. But a profitable business owner who has the capacity to hire a better-educated employee can make a substantial and sustained difference. We see the exponential value that is created when one entrepreneur taps into a market in their community and starts to grow their business, which makes it necessary to hire more of their neighbors. It's a story embodied by Morrine, a Kenyan woman whose business was transformed after she completed our Business Start-Up Training (BST) in 2017.

Before enrolling in BST, Morrine had been using a small fryer to make and sell chips (fries) out of the back of a trading center. She was struggling to take in $10 a month. She completed our thirty-day training course and started applying its principles, and soon, with an initial investment of $35, she had transformed her chips business into a small restaurant, which employed three of her neighbors. The restaurant did well and allowed her to open another new business next door—a salon and cosmetics shop. Soon Morrine was employing eight people. She added a clothing store to her portfolio and now employs even more people from her community.

Morrine parlayed a $35 investment into a set of business ventures that generates over $1,000 of increased monthly household income for nine people. In a rural Kenyan community where the average family makes less than $500 a year, that's an incredible boost, and it came from creating one employer.

Morrine can afford her children's school fees and sponsors a local orphan to attend secondary school.

TIME FOR RETHINKING

The guiding principles of our economic development program reject some of the practices that have become ubiquitous when Western organizations try to generate new income in the developing world. Anyone with even a passing interest in poverty alleviation has heard about two common practices, microloans and indigenous people making products to be sold to the West. We don't embrace either of those methods for one simple reason: we believe that they inhibit community ownership and sustainability.

Microloans have been all the rage in the past couple decades, and on the surface, they seem like a great idea. But without proper oversight, training, and accountability, the idea isn't enough. We've seen too many Westerners write checks, even in small amounts, to would-be entrepreneurs without any evidence that the recipient of that loan even knows how to run a profitable business, and the idea quickly fails. And, in the case of a new business, the borrower hasn't chipped in any of their own resources, so there's no personal investment in their not-yet-a-reality business. But the thing that irks me the most about microloans as seed capital is that they assume that the people who receive them have no resources of their own to invest. They originate from the idea that the source of the solution—the seed capital—to start a viable business must be acquired from outsiders.

We have found, again and again, that such an assumption is simply not true. When community leaders announce the opportunity for BST classes, trainees are required to come to the training with start-up capital, as little as $5, which is enough to launch a microbusiness. We teach them to assess their own resources, to start with what they have, and to multiply their earnings to grow their business over time. This philosophy keeps the personal and monetary investment squarely in the lap of the soon-to-be business owner, instead of creating a debt-debtor situation with a Western entity (or person) that may already be viewed as a paternalistic benefactor.

I don't want to paint the microloan strategy with too broad of a brush, because in some cases microloans can be a viable option. In scenarios where would-be entrepreneurs have received training and have ongoing accountability—when the entity making the loan has a reasonable assurance that the recipient has the skills to run a business—microloans can help expand a business and fuel growth.

And as for this issue of manufacturing indigenously made products to sell to Western markets . . . those ventures are predicated on a sales model that would collapse without buyers on the other side of the world. Most of the small businesses that we see spring up from our BST graduates sell products and services for which they see a need *inside* their community, allowing their neighbors to become their customers and ensuring sustainability. We take special interest, however, in entrepreneurs who sell their goods and services outside the community (domestically), because that's where economic growth is generated for the community, and it means that people within a small village aren't just swapping shillings. As business ventures grow and people can export their products beyond their small communities, significant household income growth becomes a reality.

Sometimes, in their eagerness to start an enterprise without proper training, the locals create goods that simply won't sell—not because of Westerners promising a market for their goods but because there simply isn't a market for their traditional products. When we arrived in Kwambekenya, we learned that the men were very adept at making goatskin drums. In fact, 150 men could produce four goatskin drums each and every day. The obvious problem was that there wasn't a market for six hundred goatskin drums every day, and so the men could never generate meaningful income, even though they made some really awesome goatskin drums. This is a common occurrence in communities where the people do not understand the demand side of the supply-demand equation. It's very common to see a dozen tables lined along the road with all the merchants competing for customers with the same produce items of avocados, mangos, pineapples, etc.

The BST training emphasizes the need for the entrepreneur to determine what the community values and will support. What value can be added that will distinguish the business from others? Business owners drive their own economic development by telling us what the local market needs. They might start out selling potatoes, determine that the market is flooded with potatoes at harvest time, and pivot to add value by selling chips. A key goal of our training is to give them tools and principles that will help them build on their understanding of their local market's demand, rather than push them to make something new that will sell only to strangers on the other side of the world.

TRAININGS THAT TRANSFORM

Our economic development efforts hinge on two distinct training courses: one for farmers and one for entrepreneurs. Farming and small business are opportunities that local people already pursue in our partner communities, but they could be much more efficient and profitable after they learn and apply best practices of entrepreneurship and agriculture. Through Foundations for Farming (F4F) and Business Start-Up Training (BST), we lean all the way into that overused adage about teaching someone to fish and setting them up for a lifetime.

Our F4F program originated in Zimbabwe. Early in the life of 410 Bridge, we heard about the transformational effect F4F was having on the farmers who adopted its principles, and one of our donors offered to send twenty-five farmers from our Kenyan community of Ngaamba to Zimbabwe for the course. When those Kenyan farmers returned, the change to their farms, their families, and their communities was so striking that we contacted F4F about bringing the training to Kenya. Over time, we created our own course, culling some of their key principles and adding our culturally relevant slant.

Farming is second nature in most of our Kenyan communities, but just because people have family land where they have grown crops for generations doesn't mean they are getting the most out of that land. Typically, Kenyans have a small plot that they use for

(Yvonne Busolo—410 Bridge)

A Foundations for Farming graduate.

subsistence farming, meaning they grow food just so their family can eat, and every Kenyan homestead grows the same things, chiefly maize and beans. F4F challenges them to think differently about what they can gain when they apply its farming principles to their patch of land, however small it may be.

The farmers who complete our training learn that everything they do on their farm should happen according to four key values: "on time," "at a standard," "without waste," and "with joy." The F4F course goes through the practical and spiritual reasons for each of the four standards and teaches the farmers how to apply them throughout their farming year. "On time" challenges them to plant the right crops at the right time and to capitalize on Kenya's periods of rain and drought. Farming on time means preparing their land *before* the rains come and then planting on time, weeding on time, and harvesting on time. That may seem like a basic principle, but it's a game changer for farmers when they adhere to it.

Farming "at a standard" points our F4F students to the concept of excellence. Gone are the days of scattering seeds willy-nilly and hoping for results. F4F teaches farmers to embrace standards about everything: the depth of the holes, the distance between seeds, and the amount of "chicken soup" (fertilizer) and the frequency with which it's applied. If farming is done haphazardly, the results will be haphazard, too, but farmers who keep their operation at a standard will start to see consistent and profitable yields from their land.

"Without waste" is self-explanatory, but it represents a significant learning curve for many farmers who have been working their land in the same way for decades. A key component of farming without waste involves mulching, because it conserves moisture—a must in semiarid regions. It's also important because the mulch can be created with materials that might previously have been burned or fed to livestock, such as maize stalks. When farmers save the husks from last year's maize crop and use them in the next season's mulch, they are making great strides toward the standard of using every beneficial resource on their farms. They are operating their farms without waste.

The final F4F principle, "with joy," goes beyond farmers' daily work on their land and extends to their relationships with their families and their neighbors. By reminding F4F students that they have been blessed to have land that can grow things, our instructors urge them to do their work joyfully and to let that attitude permeate every other aspect of their life. Farming, and living, with joy creates the foundation that brings unexpected abundance to our F4F graduates—in their crop yields, in their home life, and in their ability to impact their community.

Crop rotation, homemade fertilizer, and eliminating tilling are other techniques that, when executed well, improve a farmer's yield two to ten times that of traditional methods. The increase in yields creates opportunities to sell their harvest, not just consume it, and that, too, is a game changer for communities.

ARMSTRONG: THRIVING AT HOME

Like many of his neighbors in Ngaamba, Kenya, Armstrong used to do his best to farm his family's land, but he was planting on a large plot without a plan, and his farming efforts were completely dependent on the rainy season. He would plant maize seeds right before the rains, and then he would go to Nairobi to find extra work, because the yields from his farm were never enough to feed him and his family. He had three children, but when he and his wife had decided to live together, he was too financially unstable to pay for a dowry or a wedding, so they weren't "officially" married.

Armstrong's work in Nairobi was hazardous, exhausting, and stressful; he hawked eggs on the side of the road and made about $2 a day, but because there were laws against hawking, he had to arrive after dark and sell his eggs until the wee hours of the morning. It was, needless to say, a difficult way to live. When he heard about the F4F training right there in his village, he decided to attend.

Today, as Armstrong talks about his life, he summarizes it with one word: transformed. He farms full time, bringing in over twice as much money per month as he did in the days when he had to go back and forth to Nairobi. He and his wife were able to have a real wedding, he attends and serves as a leader in his community, and he volunteers with the PTA at his children's school. He has built his family a new house, and he loves getting time with his four children, especially since he doesn't have to drive back and forth to the city every night. Their fourth child, a daughter who was born after he completed the training and made so many significant changes in his life, is named Promise.

Armstrong farms on only two acres, but because he practices all of the principles learned in F4F, he yields more maize, beans, garlic, and other crops from that plot than he did on the much larger plot he worked before training. He has used his proceeds to install an irrigation system that pumps the water from a nearby seasonal river to his field and has installed drip-irrigation lines to reduce wasted water.

LAUNCHING ENTREPRENEURS

Like F4F, our BST was adapted from a course created outside our organization. South African entrepreneur Chris Black created the curriculum known as Dynamic Business Startup Project (DBSP) in 1996. We became aware of DBSP shortly after our founding, and we started hosting trainings in our communities. We saw tremendous results, but the training was expensive, and we needed to scale the trainings to impact more community members.

We purchased the curriculum, and like F4F, we adapted it to our specific context, and soon BST was one of our signature programs.

Today we run two concurrent streams of twenty-five would-be entrepreneurs in a partner community. It is a thirty-day intensive training with a twelve-month mentorship and follow-up component. The only requirement for trainees is that they come to the first session with five hundred shillings (about $5) to use as start-up capital for their new business venture. Some of the students are young people who have never worked in business before, but many have attempted a venture in the past and either struggled to make it succeed or outright failed. In either case, with that small amount of seed money and our BST curriculum, we can put them on a path toward economic empowerment forever.

Through BST, would-be entrepreneurs learn principles like keeping careful records, setting goals, adding value to their business, and treating neighbors, who are their customers, with kindness and respect. When we started offering the course, we got some pushback from people who thought that the local people in our partner communities were too poor to even afford the seed money, that they didn't have anything of their own to put into a business venture. This is the same argument folks use when they institute a microloan program. But over and over again, we have found it to be false. People can come up with the seed funding, and they often have other resources they can bring to the table as well.

Almost immediately, trainees are encouraged to start with what they have and start a business. It may be something as small

Micah Mwati training entrepreneurs.

(Yvonne Busolo—410 Bridge)

A BST graduate with her produce shop.

(Yvonne Busolo—410 Bridge)

(Yvonne Busolo—410 Bridge)

Business Start-Up Training graduation.

as three avocados or a sack of potatoes. As the thirty days unfold, students are taught to write a basic business plan and critically assess that plan with their classmates. By the time they graduate, they have commenced their business and learned what it means to be profitable, add value, and keep good records. They learn everything they need to start small and grow a venture that will help feed their family and serve their community at the same time. The training equips them to build capacity using their own resources.

Micah Mwati, our economic development program coordinator in Kenya, said that the students in his BST courses inevitably have a light bulb moment in the third week of class. Their eyes are opened to the fact that they do have something to contribute to their own personal development, and once they understand that the power to leverage success is in their hands, their potential seems unlimited.

"By the third week, things start popping up," Micah says. "Someone raises their hand and says, 'I realize I've been wasting my time. Where were you all this time? If you came when I was twenty years old, I would own an airplane!' It's a change of mindset and change of heart. I tell them to start with five hundred shillings, and they say, 'I have more than that. I have chickens, I have goats. I didn't realize I had all of these things I was wasting.'"

While BST graduates focus on their own microbusinesses initially, our economic empowerment programs also feature two programs that allow trainees to band together to create something more substantial. Our small- and medium-sized enterprise (SME) initiative supports groups of BST students who create a co-op to run businesses they couldn't shoulder alone, things like banana flour mills or fish farms. These entrepreneurs share the labor and the profits and provide yet another infusion of capital into their community.

The other group-based ventures that come out of our BST trainings are savings groups, which collect and distribute resources within a small group. Each member contributes a small amount of money (usually the equivalent of $1) weekly, and the group gives the entire amount to a different group member each week. The loans are backed by the strength of the group, and the payouts allow members to make capital improvements to their business, buy supplies, or invest in other upgrades that they couldn't otherwise afford.

EDITH: GAINING INFLUENCE AND INCOME

Edith is a great example. She has a successful retail business from her stall in the Kenyan community of Tumutumu, and she is also engaged in an SME project and a savings group with other nearby merchants.

Before she enrolled in BST, Edith was busy raising her six children, but she was dissatisfied. She wanted to find a way to contribute to her family's income. Through the principles she learned in BST, she started selling the bananas she grew on her land, and over time she not only diversified her business but also became a mentor for other merchants in her community. Late in 2020 she started a clothing business in Tumutumu's marketplace, selling the items she bought on weekly trips to East Africa's largest open-air market in nearby Karatina.

Edith's clothing shop was steadily bringing in 800 shillings ($8) a day, and she made additional income from the small business enterprise she joined with eleven other BST graduates. The group started out with a fish farm, but when a water shortage hindered that venture, they switched to pig farming. Each of the twelve members has one pig, and they share the expenses and the profits from the pig farming operation. Edith also took the initiative among the other merchants in the Tumutumu marketplace and formed a savings group to encourage the younger business owners she works alongside. Each one of them contributes 200 shillings ($2) a day, and once a week one of them receives 12,000 shillings to spend on their business. They are expected to pay that amount back to the group, so the fund keeps growing as the members upgrade their businesses when they receive the cash infusion.

SME and savings groups enable budding entrepreneurs to grow faster, save more robustly than they could alone, and do so with resources found inside their community. But the benefits aren't purely financial. The accountability, camaraderie, and mentorship are so valuable to micro-business owners. Over and over, Micah sees one class member offering expertise that can help another or one student encouraging another who lacks confidence. As Micah says, "We want to put them together in groups so that they can network and work alongside each other and add their strength to help with another's weakness."

INCREASING CHOICES

Whether it's through F4F or BST, the big-picture goal of our economic development programs is to increase household incomes to the point where people have choices. In many of our communities, residents earn less than $2 a day, which doesn't allow them many choices to better their lives. Any income has to be spent on the bare necessities for that day, and any advancement is out of the question. As Hans Rosling outlines in his book *Factfulness*, when you increase a household's income from $2 to $4 a day, a family begins to have choices. They can consider propane instead of firewood. They can choose to send a child to school or make other dietary choices. Move them from $4 to $6 per day, and they have even more choices, like installing a water tap in their compound.

We provide mentorship for our F4F and BST graduates for a year after their course ends and continue to keep tabs on them after that, and in most cases our economic empowerment graduates are significantly better off than their neighbors who have never taken the training. We have found that 85 percent of our BST graduates are still in business eighteen months after they take the course. They are succeeding with their own capital, not microloans, and often they are hiring employees from their villages. With BST, in particular, we are creating employers who are changing lives well beyond their own households.

Our F4F and BST grads are also giving back in significant ways. According to the Global Poverty Project, women reinvest up to 90 percent of their incomes back into their families and communities, as opposed to 30 to 40 percent of community investment from men. Remember Morrine, who turned her small chip business into a restaurant and a cosmetics shop? She not only pays her own children's school fees but also pays to send another child in her community to school. Often the SME or savings groups collaborate for service projects as well, paying for a different child's uniform or school fees each month.

Those efforts reinforce a key theme of economic empowerment: that it is about far more than elevating an individual. The men and women who complete our trainings graduate with an expansive view not only of their own potential but also of the possibilities that exist within their communities.

After a decade-plus of seeing the results of these programs, I'm more convinced than ever that economic development is the crucial driver in lifting a community out of poverty. But like water and education, it can't stand alone. Edwin Indeche, our agronomist in Kenya and the director of our farming programs, knows that even a highly effective curriculum like F4F would sputter if a community didn't have reliable water access or if students in his classes didn't have enough basic education to read and understand the materials.

If holistic development is tackled correctly, there is simply no way to separate one piece of the physical-needs puzzle from the others. Economic empowerment is the backbone, but water and education usually need to be addressed before trainings like BST and F4F can flourish in a community. When the goal is a healthier, more stable, more prosperous community, none of the supporting pillars can be left out of that construction process.

These four areas of emphasis, when tackled concurrently, can yield significant physical results. But . . . if you *really* want to help, it still isn't enough.

JOSEPH'S STORY

It doesn't happen every day, of course, but sometimes while Joseph is going about his daily routine on his farm in Tumutumu, a small crowd gathers just outside his property. Neighbors he knows, and even passersby he doesn't know, see the variety and productivity of the crops that grow in the front half of Joseph's compound. They often stop to ask him questions. What is he planting? Why does his farm look so much better than others in the area? Why is he growing his crops in the front of his compound, not in the back or on the sides like everyone else?

When an opportunity like this arises, Joseph takes a few minutes to invite the visitors into his shamba and lead them to the wooden gazebo he constructed next to his house where he and his family take most of their meals. He reaches for the Bible he keeps on top of a roof support, and he reads a verse or two about seeds and the harvest—a passage

(Yvonne Busolo—410 Bridge)

that draws on farming techniques to teach an important truth about God and his hope for his children.

Before he went through F4F and BST, Joseph was toiling just to put enough food on his table for his family. Too often, he had to buy food because he couldn't grow enough. No one ever noticed him or his farm, and certainly no one ever stopped to inquire about anything. But in just two short years, Joseph completely changed the way he pursued his farming, his family, and his community—a transformation that made him into a leader in Tumutumu.

Farmers are typically slow to change, and Joseph was no exception. Farmers are reluctant to alter their traditional practices, even if those practices provide minimal results. They're more inclined to continue age-old, low-yield practices for risk of having nothing at the end of the season. It's the "a bird in hand is worth two in the bush" problem.

Through hands-on training in F4F, seeing firsthand the yields at the F4F demo plot, and some strong encouragement from his mentor and teacher, Edwin Indeche, Joseph agreed to plant tree tomatoes, a unique crop for his area of Kenya. And he intentionally chose to plant his entire crop at the front of his compound so everyone who walked by could see his farm as something that's possible for them.

Joseph diversified his crops and his livestock and adopted techniques devoted to doing his work on time, at a standard, without waste, and with joy. Joseph is producing more yields than ever and is optimistic that the future will be even more fruitful. During the COVID-19 quarantine, his adolescent son even used the F4F techniques to start his own tiny plot behind the family house. Joseph reminds his son that he must do the hard work to produce a harvest, but all the proceeds from his small venture are his to keep.

Joseph's decision to plant his crops at the front of his property is working. Others in his community who are equally hesitant to change from traditional farming methods can see every day the power in F4F methods and often ask Joseph for his guidance. Every time someone comes to learn from Joseph, his own confidence grows—both as a farmer and as a community mentor.

One of those community members is a young man named Jack. It's not unusual to find Jack following Joseph around and helping him with weeding and watering. It's also not unusual to see the two of them in Joseph's small gazebo discussing what God's word has to say about life and the impact being a Christ-follower has had on Joseph's life. Joseph knows that being a community leader carries responsibility, and he's eager to teach young people like Jack that putting God first, doing the hard work, and implementing smart farming practices really can change a family.

Jack is one of Joseph's protégés. His heart is for the young people in his community. He's observed too many young people in Tumutumu content with simply living off their parents indefinitely, missing the potential of hard work and self-sufficiency in their quest to improve their lives. The traditional farming techniques handed down from their fathers leave the next generation discouraged because the yields are barely enough to survive. But Joseph is a case study—living proof—that there is a better way to farm and a more fulfilling way to live.

And even as he strives to be a respected mentor, Joseph continues to be mentored himself by Edwin when he visits Tumutumu. Edwin continues to give farming guidance, telling Joseph on one recent visit that he can catch the urine from the rabbits he keeps and use it as excellent fertilizer for his tree tomatoes. He continues to encourage Joseph to keep his relationship with God at the core of everything else he does, reminding him that the most important perspective he can share with visitors is how God is working in his life.

"Before 410 and F4F, I saw myself as just an ordinary person," Joseph says. "Now I see people looking to me as an example of what is possible. I take that responsibility seriously. Some of them just need to be challenged. I challenge them! I get to show them how changing—how I think and what I do—makes a big difference. And it will for them too."

CHAPTER EIGHT

My family's eye-opening trip to Uganda and the events that preceded it were certainly the launching pad for the founding of 410 Bridge. But there are some critical elements that haven't been mentioned that led to the surprising decision to cart my whole family to Africa to build a school. I explained the steps that got us to Uganda, but not the spiritual dynamics that prompted those events.

Before I go on, I want to pause in tribute to my good friend and mentor, Regi Campbell. Regi was one of my spiritual guides until his death in 2020. Regi was even more direct than me, and he had no room for pretension or phoniness. He used to warn against the tendency, especially within the church, to "over-spiritualize" things, covering over even mundane events with a spiritual veneer. In homage to my friend, I'll take care not to over-spiritualize, but I also can't proceed into an explanation of 410 Bridge's principles without revealing the heart of everything we do.

I am a Christ follower. I want to be very clear about that. My faith informs everything I do personally and every aspect of 410 Bridge's work. An approach to poverty that fails to acknowledge God and his work in the world is incomplete, which is why discipleship is the foundation for everything we undertake in our efforts to alleviate poverty.

Just as my friend Regi helped shape my faith in a one-on-one context, my pastor, Andy Stanley, has been influential in the language I use to express my beliefs. One of my fundamental "Andy-isms" is this: "Following Jesus makes life better and makes me better at life." This truth holds for a husband and father in Atlanta, and it's true for a maize farmer in Kenya. Another of his perennial teaching concepts, one that will help fill in the gaps I left in my Uganda story, is the idea of defining moments.

I love defining moments, and I've certainly had my fair share. Andy says it this way: "A defining moment happens when you come face-to-face with a truth that invites you to change the way you live." You can try to deny it, but you know better. You can't really hide from it, because you can't hide from yourself. A defining moment is so deeply convicting that it forces you to make a decision. It's a fork in the road of your life. The cool thing about defining moments, which is also a little scary, is that no matter what choice you make, the trajectory of your life will be changed forever.

DEFINING MOMENTS

At least three distinct points in the period before our 2005 Uganda trip stand out to me as defining moments. And even though I couldn't grasp the big picture at the time, I see now that each one of those stops along the road sharpened my focus and led directly to my leaving the marketplace and founding 410 Bridge. I intentionally brushed past these plot points the first time I told the story so I could focus on them here. This is about what God was doing to bring about an otherwise unlikely series of events:

* A SURRENDER. During the most difficult time in my life, when my business had collapsed and I had no idea how we were going to make things right, my friend Kent said something profound to me, almost in passing. He said that he had come to realize that "there was a difference between declaring Jesus Lord and allowing Jesus to lord over your life." If you had asked me back then, I would have assured you that I was a Christ-follower and had been for many years. But I had never been in such a low place before, never been so sure that I needed to relinquish control. We were deep in the throes of the dumpster fire that was our life, and I was scared, anxious, and hopeless.

I couldn't sleep one night, and at 2 a.m. I got out of bed, got on my knees, and gave up the "control" that I had never really had anyway. I prayed, "Lord, you promise the peace that transcends all understanding. I need to experience that peace. Clearly, my way isn't working. I'm desperate and have zero idea what I am supposed to do. You can have it. My life, you can have it. Just give me the next right thing to do and I'll do that. Just make it clear. Tell me the next right thing to do and I'll do that and trust you with the results."

That prayer was a defining moment. It was the moment that I decided to not just declare Jesus Lord, but to allow him to lord over my life. I couldn't begin to explain it, but after I prayed that prayer, I climbed back in bed and fell asleep quickly. When I woke up the next morning, I had the kind of peace the Bible describes: peace that transcends all understanding. It made no sense. Nothing had changed. The dumpster fire still raged. Not one of our problems had evaporated in the night. But I came face-to-face with the truth that God loves me, I am forgiven, and trusting in him would get us through. This vital defining moment came right around the time I heard my friend Dave describe the falling-down school in Uganda, and I'm quite sure that my new posture of surrender had a lot to do with my reaction to Dave's pictures. I had asked God to show me the next right thing, and when I couldn't get that Ugandan school out of my mind, I saw it as him pointing me in a surprising direction. Be careful what you pray for . . .

* THE NEGOTIATION. Despite our outward turmoil, I felt closer to God during this time than I ever had before, so when I sat in my basement office that day and "negotiated" with my Creator about when I would go build those kids a school, I was coming to that prayer/conversation from a place of trust. I was leaning heavily into God—praying, listening, trying to stay humble.

The negotiation wasn't *exactly* how I described it in chapter one. It actually came in the midst of a very intentional, disciplined prayer time. It is true that, as I prayed, I tried to make a bargain with God: "Listen, God. I know I asked you to tell me the next right thing to do and all, but here's the deal . . . Once I get my life back together, get our finances in order, get the kids back in private school, pay off all this debt, you know . . . right this ship . . . then I'll go build those Ugandan kids a new school."

The conviction that I had it backward was immediate and undeniable. And the conviction was to pursue the school now, not at some time in the undefined future. It was another defining moment. It was impossible to ignore or run from. There was no way to sweep that kind of deep conviction under the rug. I was forced to make a choice: do what he was clearly asking me to do or . . . I actually don't know what would have been on the other side of that "or." It never crossed my mind.

* THE FUNDRAISING DINNER. It's true that raising the money for the school was slow going, and it's also true that I felt like I was wearing people out with "the asking." I guess the first thing I should have prayed for was wealthier friends! But the fundraising process was also a huge faith-building experience, and when we look back on the unlikely feat of raising $40,000 to build a Ugandan school, we always return to the defining moment that came after we hosted a fundraising dinner in our home.

We organized the dinner after we had raised the initial $10,000 for the school building and committed to going to Uganda as a family, which piqued more interest in our cause. The husband of a young woman whom I worked with at the time was a gourmet chef, and she offered her husband's services for a fundraiser. If we bought the food, he would prepare a gourmet dinner for our guests. The evening was wonderful. The meal was delicious, and everyone seemed to have a good time. I had never done a fundraising dinner before, but people seemed more eager to help once we committed to going. One couple stayed well into the wee hours of the morning chatting with me and Erika. Early the next morning, while the entire family was still fast asleep, I roused myself out of bed. My curiosity about the previous evening's donations trumped my tiredness.

I went downstairs, sat down at the kitchen table, and started cycling through the checks. I'm a finance and accounting guy, which means I'm a spreadsheet guy, and I had already prepared two spreadsheets for this project: one for donations and another for the project costs. I planned to thank each donor personally after our trip, so I was meticulous about accounting for every donation. I entered all the gifts into the donation spreadsheet, and I was struck by the generosity of our guests. It was amazing to look at the total and realize that their donations would allow us to do the water project that was needed for the school and even buy other vital supplies.

Once I was satisfied that the donations were entered accurately, I moved to the spreadsheet of project costs. Again, as a former bean counter, I was pretty disciplined about tracking all the estimated costs. The spreadsheet had dozens of line items, but they were all in Ugandan shillings. I don't remember how much it was, but it was in the tens, maybe hundreds of millions of Ugandan shillings. So, I went online to find the latest exchange rate and found a long number—seven or eight decimal places. I popped the exchange rate into the spreadsheet, and it converted the millions of shillings to $27,183.38. I went back to the donor spreadsheet and saw that the total donations were $27,183.00. I blinked a few times as I tried to let what I was seeing sink in. Was the amount we needed exactly the same as the amount we raised? No way. So, I did what anyone else would do—I reran the numbers! Oh, ye of little faith . . . But the numbers were right. What we needed and what we had been given were within thirty-eight cents of each other.

In my excitement and humbled disbelief, I said a prayer of thanksgiving and ran upstairs to wake Erika. "Honey, you have to see this!"

Believe what you want about that story. It's true, and you'll have to decide whether you want to chalk it up to coincidence, lottery ticket luck, or, like me, God's providence. But for me, the point is this: I've seen too much. I've seen too much to deny God and his active presence in my life. He is amazing, loving, forgiving, and faithful. I'd urge you to simply consider that.

God blessed Erika and me with the assurance that the path we were walking was the right one, despite what those around us may have thought. There is enormous peace in that assurance. It doesn't mean that hardships won't come. They do. They did. They will. But for me, in times of confusion, conflict, uncertainty, and chaos, I'm just going to do the next right thing. We, you, all of us, know the *next* right thing to do. It might be the need to confess, or apologize, or be bold, or simply be quiet and listen.

It may be the need to stop, pause, or flee. But whatever the next right thing is, it requires action. It needs to be done, not just contemplated. *Do* the next right thing and trust God with the results. It doesn't mean that we don't plan. I'm not suggesting that people live minute-to-minute. But when things are unclear, confusing, emotionally charged, or in conflict, don't be paralyzed by indecision. Do the next right thing, as small as that action might be. But *do* it. Don't just think about it. Take a step. Move.

IT'S ALL ABOUT WORLDVIEW

Viewing the events of 2005 through this powerful lens of God's providence, changes everything. When it was happening, God's repeated reminders of his faithfulness altered the way we viewed every decision in our lives. As we were prompted to trust him with each next step and we started to see the outline of what he was doing in our lives, I became more and more cognizant of the importance and power of worldview on decision making. And since our own spiritual journeys paralleled the journey of founding 410 Bridge, we knew that this new organization had to keep a Christian worldview at the forefront of everything it attempted to do.

In my logic-driven brain, it all came down to a sort of "if-then" equation. My thinking went something like this:

- If I've really seen and experienced too much to deny God's providence . . .

- If following Jesus makes life better and makes us better at life . . .

- If the need to change people's perspectives is really at the core of any true life change . . .

- If in times of conflict, uncertainty, difficulty, etc., just do the next right thing . . .

- Then . . . we needed to shift people's worldview—from whatever it is to a biblical Christian worldview. And we needed to do that on both sides of the bridge.

As I have come to understand the vital idea of worldview, I've relied heavily on the book *Discipling Nations* by Darrow Miller. Much of what you are about to read, so many principles that have guided my understanding of worldview and the impact it has on poverty, comes from his writing, so I want to clearly credit Mr. Miller for his work.

I'm not sure why, but many people have a problem with the word "worldview"—perhaps it's because it's a word soaked in religiosity. But it's just a word. If it makes you feel better, think about it in terms of "perspective" or "the story you tell yourself to be true" or "the conversation you have in your head." Worldview is the set of glasses that sit on our nose and the lens through which we interpret the world around us. How you *thesaurusize* it doesn't really matter. The point is that ideas matter. Outside the context of a catastrophic event like a natural disaster, the reality is that poverty doesn't just manifest itself. It's rooted in the story people tell themselves to be true—in how people view themselves, their relationships with each other and their environment, and what they think about when they think about God.

Worldview drives the choices that people make. Those choices drive the actions they take, and that's why Miller says, "A worldview does more to influence peoples' flourishing—their prosperity or poverty—than does their physical environment or other circumstances." It is an issue of perception—of what we see and hear, not necessarily what there is to be seen or heard. What we think in our hearts ultimately shows up in our behavior. Our hearts shape our responses to situations, our behavior, what we think, how we feel, and how we act. Our perceptions and our assumptions of how the world works, or should work, drive the decisions we make. We make those decisions based on what we think is important in life. Those choices—those ideas—matter, and the ramifications of those choices impact us and those around us.

THREE FRAMEWORKS OF WORLDVIEW

Miller lays out three major categories of worldview. Many have distilled them even further, but for our purposes, let's not overthink it. Miller's three categories are animism, secularism, and theism.

Animism says that reality is all spiritual. The world is seen through a fatalistic lens. Any responsibility that an animist might have in this world is removed because, after all, it's up to the fates, the gods, or the disinterested or perhaps even hostile spirits. When people embrace an animistic worldview, they don't see the value in hard work, innovation, or using the natural resources around them to better their standard of living. Work is a curse, the goal is to avoid it, and it only exacerbates mankind's unhappiness.

According to secularism, reality is all physical. Secularists deny God and spirituality. Truth is relative, and secularists see mankind as nothing more than a cog in a purely physical wheel. Life results from natural, random processes. Those that see poverty through a secular lens—because they see things as purely physical and disregard the spiritual—typically look for someone or something to blame. They blame the poor for their poverty. They blame the rich, or they blame colonialism. They blame the lack of resources, infrastructure, or political structure. They blame government. They may call for the redistribution of wealth, preaching a doctrine of "fairness," but fairness is a myth and a distraction. Our focus is not on trying to define what is fair or on critiquing symptoms, but on empowering people to make an enduring difference. After all, as Andy would say, "Fairness died in the Garden of Eden."

Those who blame others for their plight begin to develop a victim mentality. They typically see life through a negative lens, believing that bad things happen *to* them, circumstances are beyond their control, and they warrant sympathy from others for all that is happening to them. They claim that they deserve better. They avoid taking responsibility for anything that happens to them, and since they think they are powerless to change their circumstances, they don't take action to improve their life.

The third way of seeing things is a theistic worldview—the perspective that there is one infinite yet personal God. The Judeo-Christian worldview attributes a person's choices and actions to what they believe about God. As Nancy Pearcey writes in *Total Truth*, "A Biblical worldview says that the overriding factor of the choices we make is our ultimate belief or religious commitment." Plenty of people will say they believe in God, but those beliefs don't have any bearing on their decisions or actions. A biblical worldview is a framework for life created not by a person's preferences or by circumstances but by God's truth.

Belief in a false god or gods leads to a false worldview. A.W. Tozer expressed the foundation of a biblical worldview when he said, "What comes into our minds when we think about God is the most important thing about us." On both sides of the bridge, we believe that people can be transformed when they think properly about God and let that understanding drive every part of their life. Ezra Taft Benson, former US secretary of agriculture under President Eisenhower, said it this way: "The Lord works from the inside out. The world works from the outside in. The world would take people out of the slums. Christ would take the slums out of people, and then they would take themselves out of the slums. The world would mold men by changing their environment. Christ changes men, who then change their environment. The world would shape human behavior, but Christ can change human nature."

FROM THE PAGE TO ACTUAL PRACTICE

It was dawning on me that a shift in worldview had to be the hub of everything else we did, and I was determined to figure out how to *really* encourage that shift. Plenty of high-level thinkers, leaders in missional concepts, have addressed the gap in worldviews, but I wasn't interested in theoretical constructs. We needed to move from the theoretical—the academic—to the pragmatic. If we *really* want to help, we had to find a way to truly influence people's worldview such that it would lead them to different choices and actions. I wasn't interested in more research or academic principles. I wasn't interested in touting the importance of worldview or writing more white papers. We had to find a way to *do* it—to actually shift how people thought. It might seem obvious by now, but the focus on worldview shift is one of the important distinctives of 410 Bridge.

So, if we're *really* going to help, worldview is the issue that we need to address. Importantly, changing to or reinforcing a secular or animistic worldview isn't going to solve the poverty problem. In fact, the opposite is true. As Miller explains, the animistic worldview leads to underdevelopment and produces more poverty, not productivity. A secular worldview limits the discussion and solutions to poverty to the purely physical or material. A secular worldview ultimately produces chaos. But a biblical Christian worldview provides a comprehensive solution to develop people and their communities. It considers God's perfect design.

Pearcey continues in *Total Truth*, "Genuine worldview thinking is far more than a mental strategy or a new spin on current events. At the core, it is a deepening of our spiritual character and the character of our lives. It begins with the submission of our minds to the Lord of the universe—a willingness to be taught by Him."

That's why we do not define poverty as a material problem. It is an issue of worldview. We may not always get it right (God knows we don't), but in the end, our ultimate desired outcome is to see a permanent shift in the story that the poor tell themselves to be true, one that places God front and center and allows them to see him working in *every* part of their lives. A biblical Christian worldview provides the truth about the entirety of how the world works, a lens to evaluate every subject matter. That, in my view, is the secret sauce to solving the material poverty problem and sustaining that solution long after we leave a community.

Bringing worldview from the theoretical to the practical comes down to intentionality. In all we do—every project or program we run—we must be intentional and purposeful to reinforce a Christian biblical worldview that God loves us, we were created in his image for a purpose, we are forgiven, we are to be forgivers, and we have responsibilities—responsibilities to be Godly neighbors, spouses, parents, siblings, teachers, business owners, and on and on.

One of the ramifications of a distorted worldview is an incompatibility with empowerment. When people have a distorted worldview, they will struggle to see their God-given empowerment to change their circumstances. Instead, they may embrace a victim mentality or believe that they don't have the agency to change. You can't empower someone against their will. You can put them in an empowering environment, but unless they claim their empowerment (own it), they will not be empowered. But you *can* expose them to the truth about God's love and plan for their lives and give them an opportunity to embrace his plan for their life. Agency and responsibility matter. Repeatedly, when people in poor communities begin to see themselves differently, when they begin to think differently, they begin to transform their reality by making different choices and taking different actions.

Oh, and by the way . . . we need a new mindset on this side of the bridge too. Just like someone struggling with poverty will never become empowered if they embrace a victim mentality, the West will never succeed in empowering people if *we* see *them* as victims, mirroring the way they often see themselves. We noticed from the very beginning that the people in our communities had developed stubborn patterns of believing themselves the victims of all manner of outside forces—tribal violence, drought, government corruption, colonialism, toxic charity, you name it. If we see the people through that same victim lens, how can we ever help them to own their empowerment? For too long Western mission organizations had been in the driver's seat, sure that we knew the right route to alleviate poverty in communities that weren't our home. If we *really* want to help, we must learn that empowerment comes only when we expose indigenous people to a new mindset and allow them to take the wheel.

STEPHEN AND SABINA'S STORY

If you were to ask Sabina about her family, she would tell you that she's married to Stephen and she is the mother of four children.

If you were to ask the same question of Stephen, he would tell you that those two facts made him neither a husband nor a father. He would confess that, like so many of the men in Ngaamba, he was a worthless drunkard—an absentee father and husband whose daily priority was to take what few shillings Sabina would make and spend them on the local brew.

Stephen can put the events of his life into two major buckets: before Foundations for Farming and after Foundations for Farming. Before F4F he wasn't really a husband, even though he had been married to Sabina for years. Looking back, the only thing he knew about himself for sure was that he was hopeless. His inability to produce

(Yvonne Busolo—410 Bridge)

enough for his family led to a lack of respect at home. That lack of respect was shared by the other men in his community. They shared a mutual hopelessness, a despair that led Stephen to conform to their pattern of the world, which was alcohol.

Technically, Stephen was a farmer like his father and his grandfather had been. He was a subsistence farmer, meaning he consumed what he produced. He grew maize and beans, just like everyone else in his village. At harvest time, if the rains came and the diseases did not, Stephen was lucky to produce ninety kilograms (almost 200 pounds) of maize. That had to feed his family of five for a year.

When Stephen's father died, his land was subdivided between Stephen and his brothers. Stephen's share was small but could produce enough in the right circumstances. But Ngaamba is in a semiarid area of Kenya, and the two rainy seasons were unpredictable and, in some years, insufficient to produce anything. Such was the pattern of Stephen's life.

This left the burden of sustaining the family to Sabina. Sabina did what she could as a day laborer or merchant to put food on the table for her family, and she was also responsible for gathering the daily water and paying for school fees for her children. Her days were long and difficult, and they were made even more difficult by Stephen's drinking and apathy.

Stephen's sea change began when he was approached by local leaders to help them recruit twenty-five local farmers to travel to Zimbabwe for four weeks to learn a new farming method called Foundations for Farming. He wasn't sure why the village leaders were asking him to help, but help he did. He assisted in visiting fellow farmers, explaining what he knew, and collecting the necessary paperwork if his neighbors were interested in traveling. Stephen didn't mind the recruitment, but he had absolutely no intention of going to Zimbabwe himself. He couldn't imagine leaving home for that long or applying himself to the hard work of learning new techniques when he spent more time drinking and sitting around than working his land during those days.

After months of preparation, the time had come for the farmers to leave Ngaamba and travel to Zimbabwe for a month. At the eleventh hour, one of the farmers got cold feet and declined the invitation. The program needed twenty-five farmers, and suddenly all eyes were on Stephen. The village leaders and Sabina convinced Stephen to take the empty spot. Before he knew it, he was on a plane. Stephen recalls, "It took three days before I knew what I was doing there. I didn't want to be there. I didn't know why I was there. And then something changed."

After those first few days sitting in the classroom learning spiritual, agricultural, and basic business principles, Stephen started to lean in. He took extensive notes. When he thought of his family back in Kenya, his own brokenness, how he had failed Sabina and his children, he knew F4F had something for him. He no longer saw his own inadequacy. Instead, he saw possibilities.

Before Stephen embraced the basic tenets of F4F—on time, at standard, without waste, and with joy; before he adopted methods of mulching, crop rotation, homemade fertilizer called "chicken soup," and soil conservation; before he deployed any of the methods of farming that would ultimately improve his yields two to ten times compared to the traditional methods, Stephen realized that God came first.

Stephen came to understand that God loved him and made him for a purpose. He recognized the grace of forgiveness. He came to understand that God gave him responsibilities: to be a godly husband to Sabina, a godly father to his children, and a mentor to others in his community.

He learned that God had made the soil and the environment to work a certain way and he was called to be a good steward of those resources. After three days, Stephen made the decision not only to farm God's way but also to live God's way. From that moment on, Stephen would tell you that his life was deeply and truly transformed. "From that day forward, I would even call home and tell them to start doing things in the farm.

"Sabina told me that I was the right man to go to Zimbabwe," he said. "The word that was brought to me in Zimbabwe was very different than anything I had received before. I caught it in a special way."

The shadow of the pre-F4F Stephen would never fall on the door of his local church. He would never have considered himself a generous man, and giving back to the local church, supporting it with the first fruits of his labor, never crossed his mind. But today he is known throughout Ngaamba for his generosity as he gives freely of his time, talents, and resources. He is a leader in his church and a mentor to the generation coming behind him.

When Stephen considers his old self, he sees a man who only did things to serve his own desires. But now his emphasis is on others—his family members and anyone who needs help in his community. The most dramatic indicator of his changed life today is the sheer number of people he mentors. He encourages other farmers who see his land thriving and want to know more about the methods taught through F4F. He encourages young people he sees on the street, youth seeking motivation, to go out and work to help their parents. He is a role model in his church, and he has even sought out the friends he used to get drunk with and seen many of them make gradual steps toward transformation themselves.

His partner in this new life, the one who best understands the hopelessness of pre-Zimbabwe Stephen and the joy and impact of post-Zimbabwe Stephen, is his wife, Sabina. Their relationship was fractured before Stephen left, damaged by a lack of trust and connection. But just as God restored Stephen's work ethic and his sense of purpose in his community, God rebuilt his marriage into something beautiful. And because Stephen has become a man who takes responsibility for his business and those around him, Sabina has found the freedom to build a vibrant business herself. The two are a team in every sense of the word, and they celebrate the fact that as they grow older, they are prospering, and that their children will never have to take care of them financially.

After Stephen completed the farming course in Zimbabwe and Sabina saw the changes in him, she signed up for BST, and through the 410 Bridge program she learned how to take care of customers, keep meticulous records, and find creative ways to expand her business footprint. She started out selling the corn, papayas, and mangoes Stephen grows on his farm, but soon she was selling clothes and shoes alongside the produce. BST, and the success she enjoyed when she put the training principles into practice, has even inspired Sabina to grow her business into other communities where she sees a need.

When Sabina remembers life in their family before Stephen went to Zimbabwe, she said she feels like crying. It's extremely difficult for her talk about. But now they are each working hard, thriving, and enjoying their life and their grown children—who are enjoying success of their own. There is more love in their family, she said, because they aren't nagging each other. Years ago Stephen and Sabina made a commitment to each other; they didn't want to grow old in poverty. They had no desire to be dependent on their adult children, but instead they dreamed of financial freedom, of the ability to help their children and support their community.

Stephen and Sabina used to be poor, but their poverty wasn't just material. As they now tell their children and the young people they mentor today in Ngaamba, they had "poverty of the mind." They had to experience a mindset shift to see the abundance and purpose that God had for them. Their minds and their lives have been transformed, and those around them can't help but take notice.

CHAPTER NINE

Changing worldview—the story people tell themselves to be true—is at the heart of everything we do at 410 Bridge. Billions of dollars are spent every year trying to improve conditions in poor communities around the world, but a scant percentage of that money goes to efforts that will actually shift people's perspectives and allow for a different way of thinking about both their present and their future.

International development agencies have their theories of change, research papers, and white papers on how to solve poverty, but these principles and concepts rarely make their way to the organizations fighting the battle or the people actually living in extreme poverty. We believe that our boots-on-the-ground approach can, and does, improve the pace and depth of development in poor communities by conveying a Christ-centered worldview. But before we delve into what that looks like in our primary program areas, we need to make an important distinction between "fans" and "followers" of Jesus.

Most of the communities where 410 creates new partnerships would not be characterized as *unreached* places. The people in these communities have, most likely, had the opportunity to hear the gospel, and many have access to church. But the more we have conversations about the challenges of their daily lives, the more we see that professing Christ and showing up for church on Sunday aren't nearly enough to make a difference in their lives. We want them to learn the same thing I learned: how to move from *declaring* Jesus "Lord" to allowing him to lord over their lives.

When faith becomes a daily exercise in putting God first, individuals and communities are transformed. On an individual level, people who had been going through life as if suffering was inevitable become radically optimistic, learning that many hardships can be avoided if they lean into God's truth for their life. On the community level, we believe that devotion to God's way can help create a community that reflects God's kingdom, a flourishing place known for compassion, dignity, generosity, purpose, and freedom.

BODIES AND SOULS TOGETHER

This picture might seem idealistic, but we've witnessed firsthand the dramatic change that's possible when people transform from the inside out. Sadly, however, even the most well-meaning churches and mission organizations often make errors in their efforts—missteps that might initially seem effective in addressing local problems but actually move a community further away from the vision of God's kingdom.

One of those missteps is the tendency to focus on only one side of the coin: physical *or* spiritual. Organizations that work in the poverty space that aren't faith-based emphasize exclusively the secular: worldly, material causes of poverty. They see people as bodies without souls. They seek to help people temporally while ignoring the eternal. On the opposite pole, and equally as bad, the faith community often sees people as souls without bodies. Filled with a desire to help people make a decision for Christ, they focus on the spiritual and disregard or minimize the physical. If they do help physically, the support is often perceived (and maybe even intended) to be conditional on their hearing about Jesus.

I love the way my friend Dr. Ravi Jayakaran explains this misperception. Ravi would say that we should not use the needs of the poor as a platform for the gospel. The gospel does not need a platform. It's strong enough to stand on its own. The reality is that the poor are both bodies and souls. If we help them temporally but do nothing for them eternally, we will have failed. Likewise, if we attempt to help them spiritually while ignoring their physical suffering, how can we claim to be followers of Christ?

THE FOUNDATION FOR EVERYTHING ELSE

Community empowerment goes beyond the empowerment of people. We seek to empower institutions as well—namely, churches and schools. It's important, therefore, that in our zeal to help we do not disempower those very institutions.

Referring again to Lupton's challenge in his book *Toxic Charity*, "To do for others what they have the capacity to do for themselves is to disempower them." As it relates to our work with local churches, that statement could be rewritten like this: To do for the local church what the local church has the capacity to do for itself is to disempower the local church. Of course, weakening the church is never a Western mission organization's intention, but as we've said over and over, good intentions simply aren't good enough.

So, if we *really* want to help, local church leadership has to acknowledge the benefits of, and participate in, reaching people outside the church walls to achieve genuine and widespread Christ-centered worldview change. How do we that? The answer comes when we open our eyes to the opportunity to advance the church in a community by integrating biblical truth into each and every community development program we undertake. That doesn't mean that church leaders have to be involved in every program; in fact, that's not possible in the early stages because so many pastors are bivocational and stretched very thin. But they are included in the planning, volunteer recruitment, and approval of the spiritual component we incorporate into our programs. They are the shepherds of their community. To bypass them for the sake of expediency only serves to undermine them and our ultimate mutual goal.

The effort to unify local church leaders, who prior to 410's involvement rarely speak to one another, begins with an invitation to attend regular pastors' fellowship and leadership development training events—gatherings designed for biblical teaching, rest, and renewal. We also share a goal to help them put a Bible in every household in the community over time. These two initiatives begin to unite the pastors, slowly at first, but more quickly as the partnership continues. As we form relationships with them, we encourage them to understand the outreach strategy and help design how they can lead and/or participate in the efforts. We educate pastors about the importance of teaching people biblical truths beyond Sunday morning sermons, in whatever way community members are willing to receive them, in order to facilitate a true worldview pivot. And we help them see that biblical principles are threaded into every single initiative in their community. We are very intentional about weaving a biblical worldview into all of our programs, even if on the surface they seem to be only about farming, or business, or education.

It's important to note that we open up all of our initiatives to *anyone* in the community, not just those who are professing Christians. We don't limit access on the basis of beliefs or perform any kind of litmus test for the participants in our programs. But once people enroll in programs that are beneficial to their lives, they also have the opportunity to hear about God's truth in a nonjudgmental setting, about God's deep love for them and his plan for their lives. As Ravi Jayakaran advises, we never use the needs of people as a platform for the gospel, but in everything we do, we put God first. We emphasize to those in our trainings that when they put God first, the lens in which they see every-thing else changes—marriages, parenting, leadership, business, farming, teaching, whatever they do. When God is number one in a person's life, they find that they work harder because they're working to glorify him. Their relationships are strengthened. They are more compassionate, more generous, and more connected to serving their community. Again, following Jesus makes life better and makes us better at life.

WHAT IT REALLY LOOKS LIKE

We consider "discipleship" one of our key program areas. Direct initiatives like pastor training, leadership development training, and a Bible in every household are important to advancing the local church. But the most significant shifts in worldview occur when we weave God's truths into every community development program. People are drawn by the prospect of becoming more successful at business or farming or shoring up their local school, and as they undertake those efforts, they encounter the living God in a powerful way. Lives are changed this way; we see it over and over.

Here are some ways that we thread discipleship through key program areas.

EDUCATION. One of my favorite C.S. Lewis quotes is "Education without values, as useful as it is, seems rather to make man a more clever devil." Simply getting more kids into school with financial help through sponsorships, keeping them in school with efforts like feeding programs, improving the quality of education by helping to hire more teachers, and building new classrooms and buying books are all important, but those measures aren't good enough. If we *really* want to help, we have to understand that C.S. Lewis got it right. The world is propagating lies to children, and we are committed to countering those lies with God's truth and creating an opportunity for children to flourish both educationally and spiritually.

The need to disseminate Christian values within schools isn't a new idea. Parents, teachers, local pastors, outreach organizations with their own sponsorship programs, and others from the West want to help children everywhere build a biblical foundation. Their efforts are well intended but often insufficient. Perhaps a pastor visits a school once a week to read scripture, or a team from an American church comes in the summer to lead a vacation bible school (VBS) for a few days. Some schools even feature a "religious studies" curriculum that takes an academic approach to teach a variety of religions.

All of those things are not, in and of themselves, bad. The adults who make them happen, either locally or from abroad, feel pretty good about themselves after they're finished. But they're not going to have the desired outcomes, because a few verses a week or an annual VBS program are just drops in the bucket when you consider all of the hours kids spend in the classroom learning within a secular framework.

If we *really* want to help, we need to do more, and we need to do it strategically. The first step is to mobilize local churches to embrace the vision for their schools and to throw their time and resources behind the effort. We seek to teach biblical virtues, experientially, using indigenous resources in the schools. We want to influence the local church's tendency to simply tell children about Jesus and then measure success by whether they make a public decision to follow him. If our objective is an authentic worldview shift, we should instead help kids discover that Jesus is attractive so that they are drawn to him. The heart of the matter is this: Jesus loves you, and he is your friend. Again . . . following Jesus makes life better and helps kids be better at life. Hearing and learning that concept at a young age is a powerful catalyst for a child to strive to do well in school. And finally, these lessons can't be taught sporadically, by visiting pastors or church members who just drop by the school when they can. We aim for them to be a consistent, regular part of a school's schedule.

In the Kenyan context, experiential biblical virtue teaching is welcomed in public schools. We're grateful for that. The program is called Discovery Kids, and it allows local church members to volunteer at their neighborhood schools to teach a fun, inter-active Bible-based curriculum on a regular basis. The lessons use hands-on activities with indigenous resources to drive home their messages, and kids who have been part of the program have responded enthusiastically. The custom curriculum teaches nine biblical virtues like cooperation, honesty, perseverance, and trust. It is a three-year rolling curriculum taught in classes four, five, and six.

We already talked about the impact of eliminating the barriers to a quality education for *every* child in a community through a different kind of sponsorship program, but when we incorporate organized, experiential, consistent biblical lessons into the schools that are already getting a boost from the other quality improve-ment efforts, the results are amazing. It's not perfect or 100 percent effective, but this type of intentionality lays a strong foundation for kids to build upon, beyond just their studies. Teachers, parents, and leaders in the community see the difference in kids who have access to that type of virtue-based teaching. They report that kids who learn how to put God first in their life experience:

- Better performance in school

- A more helpful attitude at home

- More self-esteem and confidence

- A stronger work ethic

- A resistance to negative influences like drugs and idleness

- More consistent church attendance

- Higher chance of moving on to secondary school

- Greater desire to give back to their community

BUSINESS. I'm sure that some of the people who register for our BST are a bit surprised when they show up for the first day of classes. The instructor does talk about business, but only in the context of God and God's plan for their lives. Before moving into the details of record-keeping, budgeting, or customer service, every BST student hears about the goodness and provision of God and the difference he can make in their day-to-day lives. They learn that God has provided all that they need to succeed in business. It's not heavy-handed. It's grounded in gratitude for his provision. And it's a message that sinks in.

We have more professions of faith and evidence of genuinely changed lives through BST than through any of our other programs in Kenya. Early in 2021, thirty-one people in the community of

Chembulet met the Lord through a BST course, and there are many other similar stories. God is undeniably using the biblical truths we teach to draw people to him. And it isn't just the content that has power to change lives. It's also the fact that we're meeting people where they are. They're interested in farming or business, in making more money to support their families, and we leverage those dreams to bring the gospel to people who might never have darkened the door of a church before the training.

Simply teaching people how to run a profitable business isn't good enough. If we *really* want to help, we can't just impart knowledge. In the words of Truett Cathy, founder of Chick-fil-A, "I see no conflict in biblical principles and good business practices." I couldn't agree more. Our BST curriculum is built on wisdom—biblical wisdom. Micah Mwati, who runs our economic empowerment programs in Kenya, said that there's simply no way to extricate the principles of good business practice from biblical teachings. Discipleship and entrepreneurship are fully integrated in the mission and practice of the training.

"When they come to our training, our training is wired in with discipleship," he said. "We don't separate between business and having a relationship with God; these two things are intertwined. They come to a business class thinking it's just business, but they find Jesus there. They can ignore or dismiss it, but the teaching is there. Most have neglected church, so this is an opportunity for them to reinvestigate that decision and, hopefully, go back to their first love."

Our BST participants are often surprised to learn that the Bible has plenty of practical advice for starting and maintaining a thriving business. Some of the fundamental business values we teach straight from scripture include the Bible's guidance about how we should use our money, God's instructions about generosity, and key biblical principles about loving your neighbors and relating to them as customers. Some of our trainees come to BST with broken relationships with their neighbors, and we encourage them to repair those connections not only because the Bible tells us to love our neighbors but also because poor relationships with neighbors will rob your business of its potential customers.

Another key topic, one that initially might seem unrelated to business success, is pursuing godly relationships with your spouse, children, and other family members. Business success isn't all about the bottom line; a holistic approach, grounded in biblical truth, will call businesspeople to take responsibility for their role in the family and to cultivate the most important relationships God has given them.

We also emphasize a Christian approach to stewardship, which instructs business owners to start with what they have and understand that the money in their pocket isn't theirs. It belongs to their business, so if they use those profits on themselves, they are actually stealing from their business. Being good stewards of business resources and profits also includes generosity and giving to the local church, which is an act of worship acknowledging that God is the giver of every good thing.

FARMING. F4F training has always been predicated on heart change, on challenging would-be farmers to dedicate their seeds, their crops, their water supply, and their harvest to the Lord.

Since Jesus lived and taught during an agrarian era, farming metaphors and principles are abundant in scripture. Jesus talked often about seeds as a parallel to God's word being planted in our hearts, and as our F4F participants lean in during the trainings, we see those spiritual seeds planted and growing in them as well. Stephen—who along with his entrepreneur wife, Sabina, has thrived as he has followed the F4F teachings—would never have gone to church before he went to Zimbabwe for one of the first farming trainings. Today he and Sabina are prominent lay leaders and teachers in their local church.

F4F is essentially farming God's way. God designed things to work a certain way, and those principles don't change. Our F4F participants learn how God designed the soil to work, how farmers have an opportunity to be good stewards of God's creation and in doing so restore their relationship with the environment. The key components of F4F—doing things on time, at a standard, without waste, and with joy—are all biblical virtue-based teachings.

Farmers learn to pray for their seeds as they plant, to see rain and water storage techniques as the gifts from God that they are. And like everything else in God's kingdom, we remind them that every biblical principle extends far beyond just farming a plot of land. If they do their work "with joy," that will transform their relationships with their spouse and their children, who are their partners in their farming work.

THE SECRET TO A BETTER LIFE

Edwin Indeche, who directs the 410 Bridge farming programs, said that life change starts to happen when he shows trainees what God's word says and makes sure they have their own copy of the Bible to read for themselves. Many of the people in our communities don't have a Bible and only know what they have heard pastors say, so our trainings provide a nonthreatening space for them to interact with scripture and make life-changing discoveries. Micah, Edwin, and our other instructors aren't pastors, but they are committed Christ followers who are well trained in their curricula and care deeply about the people who enroll in their courses. Because they aren't standing in a pulpit, they've found that participants feel free to ask questions about faith that they might never have uttered in a church setting.

"We take them through how to read the Bible, how to improve their spiritual lives and read it with their families," Edwin said. "Those experiences are helping us mold more and more people. We are trying to mentor them. We're not afraid of alienating them. We don't hide the truth. We say, 'This is what the Bible says.'"

This is the most vital feature of 410 Bridge's work. Without our efforts to weave biblical worldview teaching into every project, program, and initiative, the progress will hit a ceiling, and I believe it will be unsustainable. Biblical worldview teaching, when incorporated into every initiative, has a multiplicative impact. When students, parents, business owners, farmers, new mothers, pastors, leadership councils, subcommittees, and everyone else in a community are exposed to a contextually relevant biblical worldview message, we see an increase in the pace and depth of development.

When they decide to put God first, the people in the community experience an essential shift—from a potentially destructive perception of framing themselves as victims and believing only outsiders can help their situation to a positive, self-directed, cohesive, God-honoring perspective. The story they tell themselves to be true changes, and when the story changes, so do the choices they make.

LUCY'S STORY

Lucy is one of the heroes.

She was exhausted for many of her primary school years. By the time she got to school and sat down to learn, she had already been awake and hard at work for four hours. She'd fight to stay awake through class because, almost every night, she would endure a risky ordeal with her mother under cover of darkness.

When she was growing up in Ngaamba, a sprawling rural area in southern Kenya, Lucy and her family had no easy access to water. In fact, they didn't have a legal way to get safe water at all. The only nearby water source was a large commercial farm with its own well, but the company that owned the farm posted guards around the property to prevent people from poaching the water. The guards were armed with bows and arrows and instructed to shoot trespassers and detain them for several days.

But Lucy's family had to have water to cook, drink, and bathe, so they got up at 3 a.m. every day, walked an hour to the farm, and nervously gathered water while avoiding the patrolling guards. Once they arrived, they would fill their jerry cans. Lucy's mom would carry a twenty-liter (forty-five pound) can on her back and another can half that size on her side, while young Lucy would carry a ten-liter can on her back. It was hardly enough water to get through the day, but they tried to make it last until the next trek in the dead of the next night.

It was a journey peppered with danger, and not just from a late-night guard wielding a bow and arrow. Lucy remembers passing cape buffalo hiding in the brush and feeding at night. Many in her village were killed by buffalo, especially at night when unexpectedly

(Yvonne Busolo—410 Bridge)

approaching a mother with a calf. To escape detection and look for guards, Lucy's mom would walk a distance ahead of her, which left Lucy to walk alone past a huge, aggressive animal. "Only God protected us," she says in hindsight.

That was the regular rhythm of young Lucy's days, and she saw a different way to live only when she went to Nairobi for high school. When she returned to her home village as a young woman, her people were still mired in poverty and a lack of opportunity. As her awareness of the struggles within her community grew, she heard about a new organization working in Ngaamba and a neighboring village—Kiu. Lucy wanted to help her community. When she was twenty-five, she was hired as one of 410's community coordinators for Ngaamba and Kiu.

Some people throw the word "miracle" around loosely, but when Lucy considers the change that has happened in her home village, she has no other way to describe it. Her parents can now walk just outside their home to access clean, plentiful water from a spigot in their compound. Over 75 percent of her neighbors have safe water either on their property or within a ten-minute walk of their homes.

The primary school she attended, where she and her classmates used to sit under a tree because of insufficient and rundown classrooms, where they had to share a teacher with other classes, where they shared one tattered textbook among six students—that school is a different place today. Thanks to the efforts of community leaders and the investment of 410 Bridge and its partners, the school has new classroom blocks, a feeding program, ample textbooks, and trained teachers.

Lucy's neighbors see possibility now, she said, where before they saw only the same repeating patterns year after year—the same planting and harvest seasons, the same scarcity during drought, with no prospect of change. Today Ngaamba is growing and dynamic. Farmers have been trained to plant crops differently and see higher yields. New business owners are emerging because they have learned how to run a successful, profitable, God-honoring business.

The water access, the school improvements, the number of hopeful entrepreneurs and farmers who have tried new things and experienced growth after participating in 410 trainings—all of these transformations are on display for Lucy and the local LC as they continue to serve in and around Ngaamba. But Lucy will tell you that she has learned firsthand that the underlying reason for the change isn't immediately quantifiable.

"It is the mindset of my people that has changed," she said. "Romans 12:2 tells us to 'be transformed by the renewing of your mind.' I have seen this to be true. Our people will never be transformed without the renewal of their minds."

CHAPTER TEN

Every 410 partnership is designed to come to an end, an inevitability we tell local leaders from the very beginning. The goal of every part of our program is to transform life in a partner community in a way that can be sustained and even improved upon over the long term, without continuing intervention from the outside. This is one of the reasons we start by identifying local assets—to remind communities that they have the necessary resources to aid in transformation and that they will still have those resources when it's time to keep things going after graduation.

Because sustainability is at the heart of our work, we seek to communicate a few things clearly every step along the way. We let them know that the partnership will have a distinct end—that we are working toward a graduation date that will ideally come when that community has reached a series of desired outcomes. We like the term "graduation" because a graduation, or a commencement, always suggests the end of one phase and the

(Yvonne Busolo—410 Bridge)

410 Bridge community graduation celebration.

(Yvonne Busolo—410 Bridge)

410 Bridge community graduation celebration.

beginning of another. It's an end of sorts, but we hope that our communities see graduation as a launching pad of possibility as they move forward under their own power.

Think of a rocket scheduled to be launched by NASA. Before the launch date, the rocket must be prepared at one facility and then transported to the launch pad for the big event by a slow-moving locomotive-powered vehicle called a "crawler-transporter." 410 Bridge is the crawler-transporter, helping to get a community to a place that will allow them to reach heights they could never have imagined before we met.

Once the rocket is on the launch pad, of course, it flies under its own power. It's important to emphasize that when we talk about sustainability, we mean what we say. Too often, organizations confuse "being sustainable" with "indigenous sustainability" or step in to bail out people or communities when they fail to sustain a project on their own. At 410, we are committed to indigenous sustainability—the ability to maintain and continue their development with resources that exist inside their country. A children's home, medical clinic, or school that can afford to operate because of child sponsorship, or recurring support from the West, may be deemed sustainable, but it is not indigenously sustainable because it would collapse without that outside help. If we *really* want to help, we must recognize that we *will* leave at some point. When we do, have we created capacity for the people we served to sustain their own development without looking to outsiders? If not . . . if we, the West, sustain their development programs with our resources, we're doing nothing more than teaching and reinforcing dependency.

OUTCOMES, NOT PROCESS

Way back at the beginning of the road, when we are training LC members and doing empowerment exercises with new partner communities, we explain the life cycle of a partnership and quantify our slow journey toward graduation by establishing the specific outcomes we hope to achieve before we say goodbye. Our approach to setting and measuring outcomes has evolved over the years, as we have come to understand that our previous benchmarks placed too much importance on programs (process) and not enough on the actual changes that can result from those programs. We were confusing activity with accomplishment.

410 Bridge has always wanted to be outcome based, always believed that if it's worth doing, it's worth measuring. But we came to realize, in the early years, that we were measuring the wrong things. If you center your measurement on activity, on the number of programs you run, and on the number of people who attend those programs, you can find yourself on a slippery slope that makes projects, not the improvement of people's circumstances, the chief goal.

For example, we used to think that if we could get at least one adult from one-third of a community's households to complete BST, or 25 percent of households to complete F4F, then we would meet our goal of lifting average household income, because involvement in those programs would raise the community's average income level. But our measurement didn't go far enough, because it presumed that enrollment in a training would yield results. We were just measuring the number of people who were sitting in our classes, not the number who were starting successful businesses or actively increasing the yields on their family farms.

Over the past few years, we've included measuring the actual impact at a household level. We do that through household surveys and censuses, going door-to-door to get data on a statistically valid number of households within a community. We ask questions about average household income, the number of people in the home, the source of their income, and other data points so that we can effectively detect improvement in their economic outlook. Survey data is fraught with its own problems, but it's just another data point that keeps us focused on outcomes, not process.

WHEN A LEGACY CAN BE HARMFUL

The significant shift in the way we measure outcomes in recent years illustrates the danger of leaning on what I call "legacy decisions." A legacy decision is a way of operating that originated from a decision made years ago, when 410 Bridge was in its infancy. We have to be nimble, willing to adapt and rethink our principles and practices as we come to understand new dimensions of the people and the cultures where we work and form relationships. Without a dynamic decision-making process hinging on a willingness to change, we are prone to get rooted in a decision we've been making for years that may no longer be wise or effective.

As we have refined our methods of collecting and quantifying outcome data, we have also created a process for helping LCs outline specific outcome goals in those early planning sessions.

This is a vital step, but it can be tricky. When a community has little indigenous motivation and planning in the early stages of a partnership, it's hard for leaders to fathom the kind of concrete results we propose. On the other hand, if we present a blank slate to a LC and ask them to decide when we should end our partnership, they may never want it to end. There will always be something else that they'd want to do together. The outcomes might initially be hard for local leaders to visualize, but they still need to be established from the beginning—with an eye toward an end, indigenous sustainability, and the physical outcomes the community prioritizes.

SOME SPECIFIC OUTCOMES

Clear communication of specific goals is an important part of building the foundation of a partnership, but that doesn't mean the desired outcomes are the same from one community to the next. Outcome targets vary according to the specific cultural dynamics of a community, region, or country, and they are refined for each project through the Ten Seeds planning process. The outcomes that follow are general examples, but they approximate the objectives that most LCs tend to agree upon when initiating a partnership:

WATER. The current thinking for desired water outcomes is quantified by a defined percentage of households having access to indigenously sustainable safe water within some distance of their homestead. For example, in most of our Kenyan communities,

LCs point to 80 percent of households having clean, safe water within a thirty-minute round-trip walk from their home. As ambitious as this vision is, it's important to know that many communities will surpass this outcome on their own. When they increase their household income through new businesses or more efficient farming practices, they tend to install water taps in their homesteads at their own expense.

EDUCATION. It's not at all enough to talk about access to education, even if it is a starting point. We can set a milestone that aims for 90-plus percent of school-age children attending primary school, but that doesn't touch on the variable that matters more—their performance in school. As much as we would like to see 100 percent school attendance, we won't reach that goal because there are always parents who don't value education. Shifting worldviews means that we're committed to changing the culture around education, to helping families see the value in keeping their kids in school. But it's more than just access, because access alone doesn't assure a quality education. Getting students in seats is important, but so are higher textbook ratios, more teachers, feeding programs, or whatever it takes to make sure students are actually learning.

To quantify a community's progress on the educational front, we have to find metrics that reflect student learning and performance. In Kenya, for example, we define an outcome based on a school's eighth grade achieving a certain mean score on the KCPE exam. We can seek improvements on test scores, and we will also define a percentage goal of the number of kids who qualify for the top two tiers of secondary schools.

DISCIPLESHIP. Since introducing people to God's love and his plan for their lives is absolutely central to our vision for genuine change, we set quantifiable goals to ensure that people are learning spiritual truths and having an opportunity to respond. In partnership with the churches, we strive first to make sure that 100 percent of the households in each community have access to a Bible printed in their native language. Whether adults get a Bible they can understand from a pastor or kids get one from an outreach program like Discovery Kids within their schools, having the word of God in a home can make a world of difference. When they have a Bible, people are often more comfortable attending church. And if the adults in a household are illiterate, it's not uncommon for their children to come home and read to them out of the Bible, making progress toward both literary and discipleship ends.

Another discipleship goal involves our ongoing push to advance the local church by uniting the pastors in our partner communities. We aim for 80 percent of all pastors to meet in a fellowship group at least once each quarter. It's amazing to see pastors supporting each other, praying for each other, and helping each other raise money for new buildings, when just a few years earlier they were bitterly divided and competitive. Unity always triumphs, and when the body of Christ is strengthened across the community, every individual who lives there gets a clearer picture of the Lord.

PREPARING TO PART WAYS

Ideally, a community will take the initiative to tell us that they're ready to graduate from a partnership, but more often than not the LC needs a nudge to reach that conclusion. It's hard for them to separate from their perception that Western intervention is the driver for change, even when they've been powering projects largely on their own for years. We tell them how much we've enjoyed our partnership but ask them never to lose sight of the fact that *their* community, not ours, has driven the change. We might have helped them build a school building, but their kids had to study to get the grades with their parents' support. We might have provided business training, but they were the ones to start and operate those businesses. We recruited farmers for F4F, but they were the ones who had to rise early to plant and harvest, rotate crops, and reduce waste. Not only as the partnership nears its end, but also throughout our relationship, we try to remind them that it's about not what we did *for* them but what we did together with the leading energy of local people.

Without a doubt, it's scary for them to imagine flying on their own. But when we see that they're on track to meet a large percentage of their milestone outcomes, we will nonetheless meet with the leaders to start talking about graduation. We'll tell them it's time for us to move on to help another nearby community, that they have what they need to thrive without us. It's a joy to tell local leaders, "Look how far you've come. Look what you've done on your own. And look where you are today compared to where you were."

Any community that graduates from a 410 partnership has made marked progress, to be sure, but it's vital for people to understand that we will graduate a community even if they haven't achieved every hoped-for outcome. Communities graduate just like kids graduate from school—some graduate with honors, and some don't. Kwambekenya and Karogoto graduated with honors, but there have certainly been cases in which we have opted for graduation because a community was moving toward dependency. If we see an increase in entitlement coupled with a decline in community participation, we will expedite a graduation. We're not going to risk dependency just so we can achieve outcomes.

Kwambekenya and Karogoto were the first two communities we entered and also the first two we graduated, and when I return to visit occasionally, four or five years after graduation, I'm so encouraged by their continued energy, leadership, and unity. Neither of those LCs wanted us to leave, and even though we had to introduce the idea that it was time to graduate, they eventually came to see their own strength to sustain the change that was made and push for even more. They weren't the only ones who were nervous; these were our first partnerships, and even though we knew the time was right, we were a little reluctant to cut the rope as well. I remember a meeting I organized in Kwambekenya shortly before their graduation ceremony—a gathering of local pastors who hardly even spoke to each other before 410 Bridge came to town.

I remember saying, "Help me understand . . . I don't want to come back here in five years and see that this was all for naught.

You all have the opportunity in this community to continue this development, to continue to be unified. Help me understand why I should believe that this is going to continue after we leave." They quickly chimed in, telling me that they had become a very close-knit and committed group, meeting once a month, supporting each other's ministries, and preaching at each other's churches. They said, "We've made a commitment in this group that any division, any disagreement that occurs between us, needs to be settled in this room, because we don't want any disagreement between us to be a barrier for people to hear the gospel." More than seven years after graduation, that unity continues.

LAUNCHING GRADUATES INTO A NEW FUTURE

Graduation day is a grand celebration of relationships made, accomplishments achieved, and a bright future. We schedule the graduation ceremonies far enough in advance to ensure the attendance of anyone who wants to make the trip—donors and church partners from the West, 410 staff members, and other friends from both sides of the bridge who have contributed to the growth of that place. Hundreds and hundreds of people show up—families, neighboring communities, politicians looking to grab a little bit of credit, and anyone else who has walked along-side that community through the life of the partnership. The ceremony features a series of speeches from local leaders and 410 staffers, plenty of music, dancing, and a huge cake.

Since graduation marks the official end of our partnership, our staff doesn't hold any meetings, trainings, or workshops in a graduated community from that point forward. But even if the official arrangement comes to an end, the relationships endure, and because of that we still visit periodically to see our friends. It's analogous to parents visiting their adult children once the kids have moved away and started their own lives; visits are nice, but they can be detrimental when they are made too often. When we do return to the communities where we have such rich relationships and history, we are encouraged by what we find.

Sometimes we have more opportunities to interact with the leaders from graduated communities because we initiate partnerships with neighboring communities, inevitably because the people in the new place heard about the progress their neighbors had made and wanted to get in on the action for themselves. In addition to allowing us to visit our graduate communities, these situations have enabled our veteran leaders to serve as mentors and encouragers for fledgling LCs in neighboring communities.

About six months after our Kwambekenya graduation, a US team was visiting the neighboring community of Kiria. The team was led by one of our US staff. On a whim, they decided to drive by Kwambekenya unannounced, and what they found was gratifying for everyone who had been involved in that inaugural partnership. The residents were in the middle of a community workday—digging a long trench to supply water to households that had not previously had access to the safe water solution. They captured a picture of a woman about to strike the ground with a hoe, and behind her you could see dozens of her neighbors, also holding hoes, putting in labor to make short work of the trench.

KAROGOTO: IN CHARGE OF THEIR OWN TRANSFORMATION

In some ways, making the decision to graduate a community is like nudging a young adult child out of the nest. They may or may not think they're ready to go it alone, but sometimes it's the decision to cut them free that shows them what they're really made of. Karogoto was one of those communities that was quite hesitant when we told them it was time for graduation, but we are grateful for the way Karogoto has maintained strong and unified leadership and furthered the community's efforts on the other side of its 410 partnership.

Through the life of its ten-year partnership and to this day, Karogoto has been blessed with a strong, selfless LC, made up of a core of local pastors. I don't recall one moment when anyone on the LC was seeking their own agenda; through every project these leaders set the standard for what true local empowerment looks like. In 2021, I had the opportunity to sit down and debrief with Pastor James Mwangi, who served on that LC and worked as Karogoto's community coordinator. We reflected on the many ways God has worked in Karogoto, which looks like a different place than it did when we first visited in 2007.

Like many of the communities we enter, Karogoto had a serious water access issue that was forcing its women to walk many long, treacherous miles each day just to supply their family with adequate water. We helped the local leaders undertake a progressive water project that culminated with a borehole, five big tanks throughout the community, and piping (laid by the community) that now allows 85 percent of Karogoto to get water at or near their home. Pastor James remembers the unbridled jubilation the day the water finally flowed out of the pipe in the middle of the community.

"When they saw the water gush out, everybody ran here, and we had a very great celebration," he said. "It started around 4 p.m., and people went home at ten or eleven at night. People came to touch the water, taste it, and wash their face. We had one guy—he hardly ever took a bath. When he saw the water come out, he immediately took a bath."

Water access cleared the way for local leaders to address Karogoto's other pressing needs, namely, that the men in the community were drunkards, taking the money that should have been used for food and school fees and spending it on the local brew. With 410's help, Pastor James and the LC prioritized a women's knitting project that supplied women with knitting machines, training, and supplies to start making pullover sweaters for school uniforms. The Blessed Hands knitting project was designed to empower the women to ensure that food could be provided for the children. Thirteen years later, the Blessed Hands program is still operating.

The other dramatic success story in Karogoto is the transformation of the community's primary schools. The schools were severely under-resourced and low-performing before 410 Bridge came in, with insufficient teachers and a textbook-to-student ratio of six to one. It was impossible for children to learn their material when five or more students were huddled around a single textbook as the teacher shared the lesson. Add to that the

Karogoto Knitting training.

Karogoto Knitting training.

227

lack of water at the school, insufficient and untrained teachers, no electricity, and dirt floors.

Over the years, with local people driving the improvement projects and 410 Bridge and its Western church partners contributing support, schools have textbooks, and every classroom has its own teacher. The school nearest the Karogoto town center, Ngunguru, was sending only 20 percent of its eighth graders to any secondary school fifteen years ago. Today that number is 80 percent. Today Ngunguru is one of the best-performing schools in the region, a model for others to follow. Neighboring communities have taken notice of Karogoto, just as we hoped when we resolved to go a mile deep with communities, and nearby places like Tumutumu have initiated their own partnerships with 410 Bridge.

"The Karogoto you see today is very, very different from the Karogoto you saw fifteen years back," Pastor James proudly shares. "It's true that 410 Bridge and the support we've experienced have helped us, but we would not have come this far without good local leadership. We oversee our own transformation. The sense of community, the sense of belonging, the sense of togetherness, the desire to see change within your people is a very great thing for me, and I thank God that in his own divine way he connected us with our partners from the other side. We are forever grateful to him and to our friends in the US for working together with us, helping us help ourselves to transform our lives and the lives of our community."

PREMATURE EXITS

Witnessing our friends work toward tangible improvements to their communities, graduate from their partnership, and then continue to make strides is incredibly encouraging. Unfortunately, graduation isn't the only ending point for a partnership. About a half a dozen times we have had to make the difficult decision to exit a partnership, dissolving the relationship for reasons related to lack of momentum, ineffective leadership, or unhealthy patterns that run counter to our guiding principles. Exits aren't fun, but sometimes they're necessary when continuing a relationship would do more harm than good.

We actually exited one of our earliest partner communities, a "suburb" of Nairobi called Joska. That departure was facilitated by the characteristics of that place, and it was a healthy and wise decision. Joska was the third community we entered, and we were still working out our criteria for optimal partnerships during those early years. We soon learned that Joska didn't really have a sense of community at all—since it was a suburb of the capital, most of the residents commuted to the city for work, and many didn't stay there long. It lacked a single tribal bond or a united purpose, and we had a hard time mobilizing local leaders and inspiring a sense of ownership toward defined outcomes.

We did a few projects there, but it wasn't long before we realized that the prospects for unity and action were much more robust in Kwambekenya and Karogoto than in Joska. There really was no *with* in the Joska partnership; it was all about what we were doing *for* them. We decided to pull out, letting the people there know that their community just wasn't the right fit and there were no hard feelings. We didn't promote any dysfunction in our time there, and they didn't seem to miss us when we were gone.

But not every exit is as clean as the one in Joska. In several instances, we have found ourselves compelled to leave a community before we really wanted to because of unhealthy patterns that either preceded us or, in some cases, were introduced by Westerners eager to help regardless of the repercussions.

Strong, selfless local leadership is central to success, so when leaders operate out of their own self-interest, it can extinguish any prospects of authentic, indigenously driven change. We've had to exit communities because of leaders prioritizing themselves over the interests of their neighbors. When we urged the community to replace them with better leaders, they lacked the strength or the will to do so. This problem will grind a partnership to a halt and oftentimes is difficult to see early on. Before we exit, we try to either change the leaders' perspective or advocate for a change of leadership. Sometimes the unhealthy patterns are so deeply entrenched that we have to say goodbye.

It pains me to say it, but the predominant reason we are driven to exit a community early is because of harm done by well-meaning visitors from the West. We'll identify a prime community for a partnership, recruit and train local leaders, help them prioritize their needs, and then engage Western churches to walk alongside that community. Over the life of the partnership, the community will host visitors from their partner churches, and that's when things can go awry. The short-term visitors craft their own agendas for what needs to be done and how best to do it, often throwing money at the problem despite our pleas not to. In one case, a church that was working in a 410 community at our invitation actually hired one of the local leaders as their "international missionary," sowing seeds of distrust in all of the other LC members. Suddenly, the other local leaders were accusing that individual of being corrupt, while secretly wondering how they were going to find an American church to pay their salary too. It completely pulled the rug out from under the relationships we were trying to build.

The saboteurs are usually Westerners who visit a 410 community on multiple occasions and develop bonds with the local people. Some repeat visitors come to think that our development philosophy is too plodding, that they have a better plan that will get more concrete, quicker results. Teams heading over to our communities for short-term work trips are, without a doubt, the greatest risk to undermine our development efforts.

In other cases, outsiders poison the well in a community, but those outsiders come from other organizations, groups that come in and start paying local people to attend training or do development work. When that happens, the leaders we tap often lose their momentum because they're wondering why they aren't being enriched like their neighbors. Soon everyone in that community is just sitting around waiting for an outsider to do *for* them or pay them to do for themselves.

In one western Kenyan community, community participation was very difficult. The final straw was when local leaders told us that providing more textbooks for the school was a top priority. We developed a plan to fund the purchase of books with the help of the parents in the school, but no matter how many times we met to encourage them and point out that they needed to contribute, the parents were insistent that they expected 410 to pay the full freight for the textbooks. We knew they could afford to pay a percentage, and we also knew that we weren't going to move forward in that place if the local people weren't willing to sacrifice their time and money to make a better future for their children.

The impasse couldn't be broken, and so we met with the LC, told them we were no longer aligned in our objectives, and exited. The leaders were saddened by that turn of events, but they understood and had a clear understanding of their community's empowerment issues. They said that the influence from Western churches and other large aid organizations had given their people such an entrenched feeling of entitlement that they were incapable of getting their neighbors to do things for themselves.

We don't make the decision to exit hastily. It generally takes years to pull the plug, because we want to give local people every opportunity to right the ship. It's sad to have a meeting where you have to "break up" with a community you care about, and it's sad to tell a church partner that a partnership had to be dissolved because of a misstep they made on the path of simply wanting to help. No one in that situation knowingly tried to derail a development effort; in every case, they thought they were expediting it. But they were more concerned with their own process, their own projects, their own priorities, and their own time line than those of the community. Exit situations like those are powerful evidence of the fact that transformation—worldview change— must occur on both sides of the bridge.

CHAPTER ELEVEN

The necessity to prematurely end a 410 partnership because it's poisoned by visitors from the West might seem like an extreme scenario, but it is nonetheless a real consequence that can come when people from our side of the bridge inject their own sensibilities into a culture that operates very differently from theirs. It's not a stretch at all to say that entrenched Western attitudes and actions—which include arrogance, paternalism, opportunism, and reactionary practices stemming from a lack of strategy—are the greatest hazard for our work overseas. When looking to share examples of this problematic mindset and the dependency it can cause, I often think of a difficult conversation I had with a US-based organization working in Haiti.

I had become acquainted with a church that had long been linked to this particular organization. A team from the church had been on a trip with 410 and were intrigued by the difference they saw in the 410 paradigm and how their team interacted with the community. They thought their church's global efforts could be more effective if they formalized a 410 partnership, but the church's leadership was wary of alienating their current partner. Instead, they asked whether I could meet with their partner and offer some "advice." The church thought they had enough influence with their partner to create change from within, and they invited me to come up for a two-day meeting. Day one would be spent with the church and its mission-minded members and the second day with an executive from their Haitian partner. Everyone meant well, and the purpose of the meeting was to encourage healthy change, but it felt a little bit like the showdown at the O.K. Corral.

The first day with the church members was productive and encouraging. But the second day . . . not so much. From the word go, I could tell that the guy from the other organization felt threatened, that his agenda for the day was to protect his relationship with the church. He asked me to give him some background on 410, and after I gave a brief summary of our work, I asked him, "How can I be helpful to your work?" He said, "Thanks, but I think we're good."

As we devolved into an ever-more-awkward spiral, the laypeople started challenging him, telling him that his organization could learn a lot from 410's philosophy of poverty alleviation through empowering local people. "Tell him about it, Kurt," they said, and even though I had a strong feeling that both of us would rather go sit in a dentist's chair for a few hours, I went through the finer points of our history, our core principles, and our work in poor communities. Then the following exchange unfolded:

"We're very like-minded," he said. "We've seen the transformation that can occur in Americans on short-term mission trips, and we think that's of tremendous value."

"I understand," I said. "Can you walk me through what teams do when they visit that drives this transformation?"

"First they get settled into our compound," he said. "They spend half-day sessions preparing baby formula and diapers, assembling meal kits, and sorting clothes and shoes that the team brings with them or have been left by previous teams. Later in the week, the local Haitians come to the compound and the team gives out the baby items, food, shoes, and clothes."

"Where does this food come from?" I asked.

"We import it from the US in bulk, then we break it down into household meal kits."

"How does a local person get chosen to receive items?" I inquired.

"We work with a local church to identify people in need. They give needy families tickets that allow them to come to the compound."

I started to lean in. "So, the Americans on your teams, they don't get the chance to go into the community to form relationships with the people?"

"We both know that Americans, when left to their own devices, can really mess things up, so we keep a pretty tight rein on where they go and whom they interact with. Plus, we need to make sure they stay safe. They serve inside the compound."

"I have a couple of clarifying questions."

"OK . . ."

"This transformation that you talk about for the American teams, it seems to be coming at a cost to the local people. At what point, in your mind, does the transformation of the American team come at too great of a cost to the Haitians?"

At this point his blood pressure was starting to rise. "What are you talking about? We're giving them food, clothing, shoes, formula, diapers, all kinds of things. It doesn't cost them anything!"

"If I could be so bold," I said, "this transformation of the American team members seems to be coming at the cost of turning the Haitians into a community of beggars."

"You need to be very careful," he said, looking me right in the eye.

"My apologies. I don't mean to be offensive, but that's just the reality. You've been working in the same place, doing the same things, for thirty years. When are we going to stop disempowering people for the sake of some 'transformational' mission experience for Americans?"

CAN THE WEST BE WON?

As you might imagine, that meeting didn't end with a warm-and-fuzzy feeling on either side, but I am notoriously blunt and willing to challenge a backward way of doing "missions." That model of ministry is, I'm afraid, all too common, especially in some of the poorest nations. The organization I encountered that day is representative of many others that are fixated on the impact on Americans to the detriment of the people they are supposed to be helping. And it's only one example of the short-term mission paradigm that is moving poverty alleviation in the wrong direction.

All of which begs a very reasonable question: Why involve Americans at all? If their presence is potentially so deleterious to our overriding mission of empowerment and change from inside communities, why risk bringing Westerners into the picture when we have competent indigenous staff and local leaders moving things along?

The truth is that people on both sides of the bridge need each other. The West provides valuable catalytic support to the work being done. Over the past fifty years, great strides have been made to reduce extreme poverty globally due, in part, to the work of the many faith-based organizations and NGOs that have been tackling the problem for decades.

According to *Our World in Data*, "In 1950 two-thirds of the world were living in extreme poverty; in 1981 it was still 42%. In 2015—the last year for which we currently have data—the share of the world population in extreme poverty has fallen below 10%." That's incredible news!

It's important to note, however, that COVID, and the global policy response to the pandemic, is expected to reverse some of those gains. According to the Brookings Institute analysis of 183 countries, 120 million people will move back into extreme poverty (an increase of 18 percent).[1]

In addition to the measurable pre-COVID progress linked to the positive interventions, there is a less tangible benefit to firsthand

---

1. https://www.brookings.edu/wp-content/uploads/2021/06/extreme-poverty-during-the-time-of-covid-19.pdf.

engagement of the West. Even though it can easily get twisted, like in the case of that organization I encountered in the story above, Westerners really do need exposure to cultures in the developing world if their own mindsets are going to change. That exposure can take many forms, but short-term journeys still provide a fertile ground for spiritual growth, even if the sending agencies need to take care to ensure that the experiences don't exploit local people or derail the desired outcomes. Said another way, short-term trips that engage the poor are not, in and of themselves, bad. The model in which those groups engage is the underlying problem.

Obviously, organizations like 410 Bridge cannot be successful without support from the West. But we're also not going to be successful until we change the paradigm of how the West engages the poor. This side of the bridge needs to shift its perspective as much as we need to shift the perspectives of the poor, so that we aren't working against the very people we're purporting to help. This is the ever-present tension and a pressing challenge at the center of our work. Shifting the mindset starts with ending the notion that anything we do for the poor must be a good thing. It's not. It's a difficult reality for people to swallow sometimes, but we are undeniably part of the problem.

Haiti's a great example of that. We are outsiders, but years of unhealthy, paternalistic, project-based interventions have created deeply rooted dependency and entitlement there. And when we enable that by continually doing for people what they have the capacity to do for themselves, we do more to harm than to help. Turning that tide on this side of the bridge is unquestionably the hardest thing that we do.

It's imperative that we separate what we give and how we give it from our need to feel good about ourselves. We're driven by emotion and by our need to push solutions, and if we don't keep those motivations in check, we will be weapons rather than tools in the battle against poverty. Identifying and curbing those natural Western instincts is a top priority when we prepare teams to visit our communities on short-term journeys.

WHEN IT MIGHT BE BETTER TO STAY HOME

If you did a survey of one hundred North American churches and asked them what they were doing to address poverty in developing nations, a vast majority would speak first about the trips they sponsor to poor communities—trips that allow their congregants to serve the poor through construction projects, medical care, children's programs, clothing giveaways, and the like. When it comes to church mission strategy, short-term trips tend to be the tip of the spear, and when you press them for a reason for the preeminence of trips, mission pastors are likely to talk, as the man in the story above, about the transformation their church members experience when they're exposed to a different culture.

Such journeys can indeed be powerful catalysts for spiritual transformation, but if our main concern is the transformation of the short-term missionary, we are missing the mark. So much damage has been done through short-term journeys, when the participants have no understanding of what it means to *really* help.

The solution to this problem for the average global mission leader of a church isn't terribly complex. Church leaders *should* be concerned about the spiritual growth of their church members. But, in my view, their responsibility doesn't end with their church members. Objectively vetting global partners to ensure that the organization and their visiting teams are doing healthy, God-honoring work is imperative.

I take some unscientific polls on this issue when we gather global church leaders in our **410 Global Outreach Network**, an exclusive peer-to-peer network of global mission church leaders designed to help them learn, share, and network. We ask them to indicate their level of responsibility in advising, coaching, or consulting with their global partners. On a scale of one to ten, with ten being highest and one being lowest, what level of responsibility do they have in ensuring that their long-term missionaries or global partners are doing good work? Responses are all over the place, indicating that a significant number of mission pastors do not feel a need to influence the work of their partners. Church leaders who respond with a low number typically fall into two categories. They explain either that they do not feel that they are in a position to dictate to their partner how they should operate their ministry or that they see their "customer" as their church member and therefore are focused on their spiritual development through global engagement.

I understand both of those positions, and I don't entirely disagree with them. In my experience, however, we've been exposed to areas of improvement, identified blind spots, or seen the need to change some legacy decisions because of critical feedback from our church partners. That feedback is invaluable to 410 and makes us better. Iron sharpens iron, and we are all better when our church partners take a strong position on partner vetting by calling out flawed strategies or poor execution, or simply wanting to have a conversation to better understand why and how we do what we do.

IT'S ABOUT THE JOURNEY

For the record, I am a fan of short-term journeys. A big fan! The positives far outweigh the negatives. The tricky part is to address the potential issues and unintended consequences that come from doing short-term trips poorly. In a poverty context, here are some of the ways short-term mission trips can work against the very people they claim to serve:

COMING IN WITH A "SAVIOR" COMPLEX. This was the point I was trying to make that day at the church meeting with the Haitian organization. I felt increasingly disheartened at the approach of the established mission organization that only saw interactions between Westerners and local people when the locals came to the gates for handouts. This issue is linked to a false perception of the poor. In order to help the poor, we must change how we see the poor. Any view that the poor are victims or incapable of helping themselves prevents us from empowering them and preserves the false notion that they must continually look to outsiders to pull themselves out of their circumstances.

MISSING OPPORTUNITIES TO BUILD RELATIONSHIPS. This was my own major misstep on that long-ago trip to Butalale, when I was determined to build school walls to the exclusion of anything else, while Erika was in the community every day getting to know the people, hearing their stories, and understanding their struggles. If the top priority of a journey is based in Western action (building something, leading a program we bring from home, doing *for* people rather than *with* people) but it fails to create time to truly connect in an effort to create trusting relationships and share their faith journeys, then the trip isn't a *mission* at all.

PLAYING FAVORITES. It's an unfortunate but common story—our relationships tend to mask our objectivity. We genuinely like the people we connect with in country. That's great. I hope so! But, all too often, those relationships tend to become more important than the accountability and impact we need to see. A Western church starts sending teams to a certain community, and in their efforts to involve the local church, they become connected with one particular church. Soon every work project from the Western church is being run through that one pastor, and, in some cases, the overseas pastor even ends up on the Western church's payroll. The Western church feels good about their "trusted" inside track to the community that they're trying to help, but what they don't see is the potential damage and disunity this approach has on the other pastors and churches in that community. It often perpetuates the indigenous perspective that they must find their own Western benefactor if they want to keep pace. This approach isn't always unhealthy, but more often

242

than not, I've seen it undermine any chance of a collaborative, unified, noncompetitive approach from *within* the community.

I remember a conversation I had with a US global missions pastor. He reluctantly shared his experience with a bivocational pastor (Julio) in the Dominican Republic who had planted a church just inside the city's massive garbage dump. Julio worked as a landscaper during the week and pastored his church at night and on weekends. His church was literally inside the city garbage dump when they met and began supporting his ministry. Needless to say, his church body was very poor. Julio had a vision of moving his temporary church from inside the garbage dump to just outside where he could build a permanent facility and attract a larger congregation. The American church wanted to help him build a new, bigger, better church but also recognized that Julio's time was being diluted by his day job as a landscaper. Soon the American church convinced Julio to leave his landscaping job and move to full-time pastor. The US church would take him on as a global "partner" and pay him a salary.

The problems began when Julio, almost overnight, became one of the wealthiest men in his very poor community. His American church partner helped him purchase a plot of land and build a nice new church and started to pay his salary. This began to fracture any unity that could have been forged among the other pastors in his community and, more importantly, began to create an unwillingness for his church body to support him financially. And all the while, Julio's American partner was oblivious to these new dynamics. American teams would visit Julio's church, and no one was the wiser because no one was asking the hard questions.

And then, as will *always* happen, the American benefactor went away. This could happen because of a change in the church mission's leadership or a shift in their mission's strategy. Or it could result from an inability to financially sustain the relationship. Whatever the reason, it will invariably happen and relationships will end—in this case, with Julio and his church. It didn't occur overnight, because the American partner understood they needed to withdraw over time. But as the supporting church tried to wean Julio off their financial support, they found that the congregation was reluctant, or unable, to tithe enough to support Julio's full-time ministry and sustain the church infrastructure that had been created. The years of American support and the consistent stream of American visitors led the church body to become apathetic with their scarce resources. Three years after they ended their partnership, Julio's church failed.

This problem isn't limited to pastors either; some organizations put other local leaders on the payroll for a range of reasons, but the result is almost always destructive. In Haiti local people will warn each other: "Stay away from my *Blanc*," translated as "my white." Their meaning is "That's *my* benefactor and you had better stay away. Find your own Blanc so my Blanc's generosity toward me isn't diluted when he or she also tries to help meet your needs."

LEADING WITH PROJECTS. It's a common refrain—communities will find some building for a visiting work team to paint, repair, or improve. They present the same school or wall to the next team, and the next, until it's thick with paint, or a new mural, or whatever. Eager to please, the leaders in poor communities will find any old project just to make Westerners happy, but its completion rarely makes a ripple in that community's poverty problem. Or the Western team decides on its own, like I did with Butalale, that their services are needed for a school construction, or a water project, without finding out what is already going on in that place and whether their particular pet project is even really needed.

Years ago, a team of well-wishers visited a remote part of Kenya. They came face to face with the need for permanent housing and compost latrines, and they resolved to improve that community's housing and sanitation conditions. They went home and raised the necessary funds to build small but sturdy houses and a large compost latrine facility. The local people expressed their gratitude, the Westerners felt great about helping, and they flew back to the US. A few years later, someone from that team returned to Kenya, visited that community, and found cows living in the homes and the compost latrine completely unused!

The people valued the safety and security of their livestock to such a degree that it was better for the cows to live in the houses while the people lived outdoors. As for the compost latrines . . . the people had an approach to "doing their business" that was drastically different from American sensibilities, but they were satisfied with it. No one ever took the time to meet with local leaders, understand their most pressing problems, and ask whether they even wanted a new latrine. But the cows were comfortable.

Failing to call visits what they really are. This is more than just semantics. Labels matter. Nearly every church tells their teams they're going on a short-term "mission" trip, but are they? A mission trip should always feature robust opportunities for evangelism or discipleship. Some churches say they're doing missions, but what they're really sending are "service" teams or "vision" trips. There's nothing at all wrong with service or vision trips, but participants on both sides of the bridge need to have intentionality and clear expectations of what will and won't happen during that week to ten-day period.

This goes back to the truth that in ministry or outreach, we often see either souls without bodies or bodies without souls. In the first instance, souls without bodies, a church might send a trip that is purely missional, focused only on soul saving and discipleship with no regard for the physical needs in the community. If people are seen as bodies without souls, work teams will come and *do*—building, painting, digging—without ever taking the time to just *be* with the people. Like Jesus did in his own ministry, we need to have the highest regard for both the body and the soul.

RETHINKING SHORT-TERM JOURNEYS

But despite the drawbacks, the benefits of short-term journeys are clear. The Bible calls us to go and make disciples and commands us to serve the poor, and trips can help believers fulfill these commissions while helping to make a real impact across the globe. Trips are still valuable with a big caveat: they are valuable if they're done well. We approach the training and implementation of journeys very differently from most sending organizations. These are some of our guiding principles for short-term journeys:

GO ONLY IF INVITED. We don't just assume a community wants an American team to show up. The people in the communities we serve are incredibly welcoming and generally love to roll out the red carpet for visitors, but their commitment to hospitality requires considerable time and energy. There have been times when one of our church partners has proposed a trip, but when our local staff asks the LC, they learn that it's harvest season, so the local people don't have the capacity to host. Or they have just had a big event or project and they're a bit worn out. It's rare for communities to say no to a visiting team, but from time to time they do say, "No, thank you. Let's find another time." We absolutely respect their right to do it; it's another way to confirm that we're coming alongside them as we co-labor to improve their community.

JOIN THE COMMUNITY IN WHAT'S ALREADY HAPPENING. Teams from the West shouldn't be the initiators of activity. They should consider themselves guests and co-laborers, showing up to assist with whatever is already happening. When this is handled well by the visitors, teams can be a catalyst, giving a spark to local people whose energy for the work might have started to wane. We hear communities say things like, "If Americans can leave their homes and come all this way to help us, surely we can give more time and effort ourselves. After all, it's our community." They want to prove to the visitors that they have the vision and the drive to make things happen for themselves.

If someone were to call us and say, "We've got a bunch of quilters in our congregation who want to go over to teach Kenyans how to quilt," we are likely to say no to that idea unless we have a community that has already expressed an interest in a quilting co-op or similar project. We don't create itineraries based on American interests or agendas. Teams need to understand that they're just one piece of a large mosaic in the community they visit. There are a bunch of things that happened before they got there and a bunch of things that are going to happen after they leave. They're plugging into a short window of time in the lifeline of that community's development.

It's vital that our teams understand that they're just one point on the time line for the communities they visit, so that they don't sabotage that big picture with a few rash decisions while they're in the community. Giving away clothes or money, making bold promises about things that might happen in the future, exchanging contact information—all of these actions can threaten the foundation we've already laid and undermine our future work in a place.

RELATIONSHIPS, RELATIONSHIPS, RELATIONSHIPS. In our pre-trip training materials, and every day our teams are in country, we tell visitors the same thing repeatedly. Put the paintbrush, shovel, or chalk down and grab the person working next to you and go sit under a tree. Ask them about their life, their family, their work. Ask them what daily life is like for them. And share your own story with them. I missed so much when I was head-down, slinging cement in Butalale. I missed the chance to be inquisitive and curious, to be changed by the faith walk and culture of a new friend in a place across the globe. I totally missed it, and I promised myself I would never miss it again. We're not going to create an environment where hundreds and hundreds of people a year go to serve God's kingdom and miss the chance to form relationships that are authentic despite being temporary. The relationships are where God does his best work.

Potentially life-changing relationships also happen between members of a work team and between the team members and their leader. The Western team leader's role is to focus on their people and the heart change that's happening on the trip—helping them process what they see every day, helping them recognize God at work, and providing care and discipleship. Since the team is helping with an ongoing project, the Kenyan host who is serving as point person for that team will handle the projects and day-to-day logistics.

And then there is the impact that we rarely see or hear about. I was at my home church one Sunday and a man was being baptized. As part of his baptism, he made a quick video of his testimony. To my humbled amazement, he explained how he had gone on a 410 Bridge trip to Kenya and how it radically changed his relationship with his Heavenly Father. He met people who taught him more about God's love, grace, provision, and faithfulness than he could ever have taught them. A faith-building journey like that is worth all of the potential risks.

Most importantly, we try to create intentional opportunities for our in-country hosts to disciple the American team. We want to enroll them in the discipleship process and not see themselves as mere recipients, but contributors. This is a very powerful opportunity for the people living in our communities to participate in what God is doing in the hearts of the visitors. We sheepishly explain that we are about to put a group of selfish, arrogant, materialistic, and entitled Americans on a plane and send them their way. We ask them whether they would be willing to disciple our people. Would they be willing to show them what it means to have true community—something we seem to have lost on this side of the bridge? Would they show them what it means to have joy in the midst of having nothing? Our friends literally sit up in their chairs and welcome the responsibility. It empowers them to be part of the Kingdom-building solution, and they are excited to help because, after all, they see the brokenness in us that we do not see in the mirror.

Since changing worldview on both sides of the bridge is really our number-one priority, we approach journeys with the belief that we serve most effectively, and experience the most transformation ourselves, when we have firsthand involvement with the people whom we serve. We don't want to help the poor without knowing the poor, and if done well, journeys provide an excellent means to understand poverty through authentic relationship.

THE RIGHT KIND OF STRATEGY

Since churches are so often the senders of short-term teams, pouring into church mission leaders can go a long way toward changing the philosophy and practice of global missions to the poor. A key part of shifting the short-term mission paradigm and helping trips be a positive, not detrimental, influence on the poor is by taking a hard look at a church's global strategy—or, all too often, the lack thereof. Through the *410 Global Outreach Network*, we've had the opportunity to talk with many global mission leaders who really want to help the poor but lack the focus and efficacy that come from creating and adhering to a well-defined mission strategy. Unfortunately, many churches engage in global outreach using a "strategy" that seems like it was made by tossing darts at a world map.

It's not enough to say that strategy involves sending people to one place on every continent, as if the church is a travel agent trying to hit a variety of places around the world. It's also not enough to say that strategy is driven by enthusiastic constituents who have a passion for a particular project or person somewhere on the planet. Without a defined, measurable strategy, we become rudderless and subject to mission drift. Global missions shouldn't be dictated by the changing whims of staff or lay leaders, no matter how admirable their intentions might be. With impulse-driven mission practices, a church's mission staff misses the opportunity to craft an approach that helps fulfill the big-picture mission of the entire church.

The ***410 Global Outreach Network*** was formed to allow an expansive network of global mission leaders from North American churches to share best practices, discuss challenges, and meet the challenge of sharpening their global mission strategy in a peer-to-peer environment. One of my personal passions is to see the North American church unify and form a more refined understanding of why and how they engage with the poor in other nations. As we facilitate these conversations, it's our desire to simply help churches get better at global outreach.

LET'S HOLD UP THE MIRROR

Remember, we're talking about a wholesale worldview shift on the Western side of the bridge, one that is just as crucial to poverty alleviation efforts as the changes of perspective happening in countries like Kenya and Haiti. North American well-wishers must be open to a radical new way of thinking, one that requires them to take a back seat and trust indigenous people to take the lead in their own transformation. When our minds have been transformed in this way, we'll be attuned to attitudes and practices that run counter to serving *with* instead of *for* the poor. And, frankly, we should be willing to call it out when necessary, like some were compelled to do recently in a group chat dedicated to organizations and missionaries doing work in Haiti.

Haiti was in the grip of major civil unrest and in the aftermath of a catastrophic earthquake in 2021, and I was reading the messages on a What's App channel expressly created for organizations trying to serve in that struggling nation. One of the members, an

American stationed in Haiti, posted about the danger she felt she was in and urged everyone to write letters to the White House, the US State Department, the American Embassy in Haiti, and anyone else who might be able to orchestrate the movement of US troops to Haiti to help restore peace and security. She wrote, "It is not an exaggeration to say that missionaries are the heart and soul of Haiti." She went on to use that phrase as justification for US intervention to restore order and keep the outsiders working in Haiti safe.

And therein lies the problem: missionaries are not the heart and soul of Haiti; the *people of Haiti* are the heart and soul of Haiti. She had completely discounted the idea that by helping empower local leaders and encouraging a change in worldview, the Haitian people could move toward taking control of their own destiny. When we continue to point to outsiders as the primary source of the problems in nations like Haiti—and, even worse, point to outsiders as the primary source of the solutions—we simply reinforce a worldview that the local people are incapable of fueling their own development. We reinforce a victim mentality that takes them further and further away from empowerment.

If you've hung with me this long, you've read for yourself that I'm not driven by emotion, but I am passionate about *really* helping the poor. I am driven by a genuine calling to see the West aid in *actual* transformation, not play-acting that makes us feel good and leads to no discernible life change for people trying to live on less than $2 a day. That's the spirit and the desire embedded in these final words.

So many people in the West say it, and I think they mean it: they *really* want to help. So if we *really* want to help, pause . . . analyze, think critically, hold up a mirror, repent, and commit to change—strategically and tactically. Good intentions just aren't good enough. When are we, the Body of Christ, going to resist the old, tired methods that are more about what *we* want to do than actually achieving the outcomes we seek? If we do, we can pivot to a different way, a way fueled by changed worldviews that lead to local empowerment and, ultimately, real transformation and the end to extreme poverty.

ALLOW ME TO END WITH THIS . . .

I asked the 410 Bridge in-country staff to imagine that they were in a room full of Western donors and well-wishers, people who had the capacity and desire to help. All of the donors *really* want to help, and they want to hear directly from people doing the work. I asked them, "If you were free to finish the following two statements, what advice would you give to the room full of Western donors?"

"If you really want to help, start _____."

"If you really want to help, stop _____."

You will find some of their responses convicting.

I'll go first:

> . . . stop defining poverty as a material problem. Define it as an issue of worldview.

> . . . start defining development as what people do for themselves.

> . . . start allowing them to lead. You follow.

> . . . start separating what you give, and how you give it, from your need to feel good about yourself.

> . . . stop viewing the poor as a set of problems to be solved. They are the solution.

> . . . start making the local church the hero.

> . . . stop measuring success by what you do but rather by what the people do on their own.

KENYA STAFF

Dr. Claire Nyambati—Kenya Program Officer

> . . . start by asking what I am doing with what I have.

> . . . stop thinking you have the answers to everything.

Jacob Njagi—410 Kenya Board Member

> . . . start by engaging the community before doing projects.

> . . . stop taking the lead.

Rev. James Mwangi—Karogoto Leadership Council

> . . . start by organizing a strong group of indigenous leaders.

> . . . stop thinking you have all the answers.

Micah Mwati—Economic Development Program Coordinator

> . . . start addressing the people's mindset.

> . . . stop just doing projects.

Edwin Indeche—Agronomist/Foundation for Farming Program Coordinator

> . . . start investing in indigenous leadership.

> . . . stop giving handouts!

Crispoh Molel—Community Coordinator/Savings Group Program Coordinator

> . . . start walking *with* the poor.

> . . . stop doing *for* the poor.

Jack Silange—Community Coordinator

> . . . start transforming the mind.

> . . . stop spoon-feeding people!

Benjamin Mambo—Education Program Coordinator

> . . . start assessing the assets before needs to properly identify community priorities.

... stop when they are empowered.

Fred Mwashimba—Logistic Manager

> ... start believing that the poor have solutions to their problems.

> ... stop thinking that you are the solution to their problems. They understand their problems better.

Patrick Odino—Accounts Manager

> ... start with indigenous leaders.

> ... stop thinking that there is somebody else who will help.

Maggie Njue—Health and Wellness Program Coordinator

> ... start supporting the poor with what they are already doing.

> ... stop introducing something new without first training them.

Lucy Jackson—Child Sponsorship Coordinator

> ... start at where the community is and with what they have.

> ... stop at the point where they get it and are empowered.

Samson Mwangangi—Discipleship Program Coordinator

> . . . start opening up the minds of the poor to understand they can come out of poverty, because poverty is a mindset issue as a result of broken relationships.

> . . . stop once the solution to a problem is resolved. Do not continue to help.

Victoria Mutua—Community Coordinator

> . . . start applying the right tools to the prioritized problems.

> . . . stop once the problem is resolved. Do not overstay your welcome.

Dorcas Mbaria—Community Coordinator

> . . . start educating the community.

> . . . stop changing priorities based on your definition of events.

James Gitau—Community Coordinator

> . . . start teaching them to fish, providing skills to resolve their problems without you.

> . . . stop once they can sustain themselves.

Lucas—Community Coordinator

> . . . start providing education and training to eradicate illiteracy.

. . . stop helping without using a proper channel of communication through leaders.

Shadrack Musili—Community Coordinator Manager

. . . start training on shifting the mindset/worldview.

. . . stop all unhealthy giving!

Kahuria Leadership Council

. . . start with involving community leaders.

. . . start with prayer.

. . . start using the gifts that already exist in the community.

. . . stop after accomplishing the objective.

. . . stop projects that cannot be sustained without you.

. . . stop when it's time to stop. Do not overstay your welcome.

Kiu Leadership Council

. . . start being patient.

. . . start ensuring that the need is coming from the beneficiary, not you.

. . . start identifying the available resources in the community and provide education on how those resources are useful, no matter how little they are.

. . . stop once the goal is achieved and stop giving directly
to individuals.

. . . stop when the party can do the upliftment by
themselves.

. . . stop once individuals' minds have opened and they
realize how what they have is helpful and how to
multiply it.

Ndibai Leadership Council

. . . start maximizing local resources without wastage.

. . . start by building relationships to determine what the
other party is really going through.

. . . start with the end in mind, setting targets for the work.

. . . stop helping in ways that the community cannot sustain
on their own.

. . . stop helping after the need has been addressed.

Mugaa Leadership Council

. . . start empowering by providing skills through training.
They will be able to work for themselves without
depending.

. . . start to understand their priorities before providing
donations.

... start empowering the needy party to understand that they have capabilities of solving problems by themselves.

... stop once the objectives have been met.

... stop once the party is empowered to sustain themselves.

GUATEMALA STAFF

Felix Camposeco—Country Director

... start by recognizing the blessings that God has already provided to solve their own problems.

... stop thinking that what you believe, and what you want to give, is what they really need.

Jeremy Barth—Community and Economic Development Coordinator

... start by asking God for some humility.

... stop thinking of shallow, short-term solutions. Short-term solutions often become long-term problems.

Liliana Escobar—Hospitality

... start focusing on the attitudes of the people instead of wasting resources on unnecessary programs.

... stop thinking you are going to change the world with your unnecessary programs.

HAITI STAFF

Crizauld Francois—Country Director

> . . . start listening and observing more and talking less.

> . . . start arming community leaders with skills that can transfer to future generations.

> . . . start with building trusting long-term relationships.

> . . . stop seeing the poor as less smart, lazy, and beggars.

> . . . stop thinking of short-term involvement only when natural disasters happen.

> . . . stop thinking that you have the solution for every problem.

> . . . stop thinking that your way is always the best way.

> . . . stop thinking that more money and more resources can bring better solutions.

> . . . stop bringing canned projects done elsewhere.

> . . . stop thinking that more wealth means more happiness.

Stania Joujoute—Executive Assistant and Hospitality Manager

> . . . start partnering with organizations that work directly with locals and are indigenously led.

> . . . start focusing more on development effort than relief effort.

. . . stop funding projects that are not wanted by locals.

. . . stop thinking that you are the solution to the problems.

Fenold Appolon—Human Resource Manager

. . . start changing people's behavior and understanding because they can, in fact, change their conditions without you.

. . . stop thinking only about your existence and only what you think will be helpful.

Ishtar Pady—Sponsorship Program Coordinator

. . . start recognizing that private efforts can have significant impact only if reinforced with public efforts and vice versa.

. . . stop thinking of development in a purely Eurocentric/ American way. The focus should not be on what they have, or what you think they should have, or how they live compared to your context.

Jean Samuel Alteus—Program Coordinator

. . . start encouraging them to participate in decision-making and their own development.

. . . stop reinforcing people's belief that outside donations are the only way. Safeguard their dignity.

Leon-Enos Jean—Economic Development Program Coordinator

> . . . start mobilizing children for lasting change. They are the leaders of tomorrow.

> . . . stop providing direct support to adult community members.

> . . . stop short-term interventions.

BACKWARD

I love Kurt's book, but when he asked me to write a forward, naturally, I declined. I did, however, agree to write the "backward" since these next few pages will go back in time and provide the genesis of a fascinating story.

It seems like a few lifetimes ago when I stepped off a plane for my first experience in a country struggling with extreme poverty. I had no idea what my first trip to Africa would hold. I was embarking on a journey that would have more twists and turns in it than I could have ever imagined. It would be a catalyst for people and stories in that country and in the US. As you read Kurt's book, you'll get to engage with some of those people and their stories.

A few months before this, I had walked through my living room and glanced at the television. Oprah was telling a story about how her heart and soul had been captured by her recent trip to Africa. I found myself captivated. Oprah is a master storyteller, and her video clips seemed to add some exclamation points and a few question marks to every sentence that came out of her mouth. I'm not sure why I was so captivated. I'd seen countless shows and stories about kids in other countries. I'd worked with some well-known artists and musicians who had worked with large global nonprofits. They were all trying to make a difference in the lives of people in godforsaken places all around the globe.

I was never particularly interested in getting on a plane to anywhere outside of the good ole USA. I was glad there were people out there doing good things for the people on the other side of the world, but I was certain I wasn't one of them. The next few days were disturbing. I couldn't get those images and Oprah's stories out of my head. We've all heard the phrase "voices in your head." The ones I was hearing were loud and relentless. It wasn't anything specific. Just, "Hey …! You …! Don't forget that show. Go do something." I kept thinking, "What in the world would I do?" I'm a comedian. An event producer. An emcee. I create stages and conferences and interrupt my pastor on Sundays to make people laugh. My college roommate used to tell me I was built for comfort. He wasn't wrong. I heard lots of stories from people who headed to foreign lands. Before you go, you have a long list of things to prepare for, starting with applying for a passport. Oh yeah, and there is the matter of getting shots. And not the kind you get at a bar, though some liquid courage may be needed before getting jabbed for typhoid, yellow fever, tetanus, and the rest. I'm not a coward about that stuff (OK, maybe a little), but my skin covers my body to protect what's lying underneath. I'm good with that, and I'm not terribly fond of watching

266

something containing a disease be stuck through that protective covering.

More voices in my head about that and a litany of other stuff, from the water, the bugs, the food, and, of course, there is the eighteen-hour plane ride. And even if I did go, what would be the point?

I could write a book about everything that the two sides of my brain argued about, but this is the "backward" to a much more important book than all that.

I've learned in my life that if I listened to the more ridiculous side of my brain, I usually was pretty excited about the eventual outcome of whatever that ridiculous side argued for. Weird, I know. I also realized a long time before that, that if I just dreamed a little and asked the question, "What if . . . ," well, you'll hear more about that as you read Kurt's book.

Within a week of watching Oprah, I called some friends who were trip organizers and asked whether they could take me and some interns to Africa They said no. It was too late in the season to make that happen before the summer. That answer wasn't acceptable, and within another week we were making plane reservations.

Another interesting aside to this story . . . I couldn't picture being on a plane for that long or traveling bumpy dirt roads because I was in a pretty rough season after a few spine surgeries. I literally had to carry a seat cushion with me everywhere I went. The seat cushion helped for a few hours, but after that, I had to stand. So, wait . . . how long was this flight?

I was acquaintances with another gentleman who struggled with even worse back pain than me, so naturally, I figured he should accompany me. When I told him I thought he should go to Africa, he laughed. He had the same thoughts I had. The trip was too long, too painful, and what would be the point? But he graciously agreed, and there we were, two guys carrying their butt pads, leading a small group on a painfully long trip to Kenya.

OK, fast forward . . . The trip blew the minds and broke the hearts of all of us who went.

If you've been on a trip like this, you know why. If you haven't, well . . . you need to go and find out for yourself.

On the long trip home, when it no longer mattered that we had sciatica or surgery scars, my mind raced with ideas that kept me awake and disturbed. Somewhere around maybe 4:00 a.m. in some time zone, I drew a diagram and some ideas on a napkin and hobbled back to my friend lying in the aisle of the plane and showed it to him. He happened to have a lot of money and was always very generous. After I explained to him what I was thinking, he said, "OK, if you do that plan right there on that napkin, I'll help you get started."

Now I was stuck. I knew I didn't have the gifts or the discipline to do what needed to be done. I just knew that I had some ideas. So, now what?

That's where the author of this book comes in . . . my friend Kurt.

At the time I didn't know Kurt from Adam. He called me, and we met for dinner. From that point forward, both our worlds began to turn upside down.

I knew that if any of these ideas were ever going to get off the ground, someone else was needed. A leader, a thinker, a disciplined executer. An honest and trustworthy human being.

A risk taker. An innovative thinker willing to consider ideas that my crazy brain came up with and the strength and courage to tell me that I'm out of my mind. Someone who would work for a fraction of the money he was worth. A person who could take a fragment of an idea and make it better.

That was a big ask.

That is Kurt!

It's been a lot of years now since we met and started talking about "what ifs . . . "

The evolution of this organization, 410 Bridge, has been astounding. There have been hurdles that would have tripped up great leaders. If those hurdles were too high for Kurt, he'd figure out how to go around them . . . or under them . . . or through them . . . or simply power the hurdles out of the way. In building this bridge, he and his team have built a foundation that can change the future of the global poor, one community at a time.

Kurt understands that it's the stories of individual impact that change hearts, but it takes a brilliant overall strategy to make a lasting difference. As you read *If You* Really *Want to Help*, you'll be captured by the stories while you get a clear understanding of the paradigm-shifting strategy.

As I read his book, I was captivated. It brought back a lot of memories.

Kurt just knew how to make things happen in incredibly difficult environments. Things that nobody else I know could have done. And they were always better than anything I could have thought of. It's not my intention to make this about Kurt. I just want you to know what kind of man wrote it. He's definitely human. And that means he had to change how he thought, worked, and led in order to keep the organization effective. But what impresses me about Kurt is that he knows this about himself. He recognizes his faults and works hard on them. That's the sign of a great leader. The thoughts and ideas inside the head of that good leader are what you get to read about here.

If you're a leader, you will want to read this book because it will help you think more like a leader. If you are a person who wants to help make a difference in the world, you should read this book because what we usually think about when we think about helping in the world is too often bass-ackward and we need to know how to change our thoughts on almost all of that. (*Kurt'll probably edit out that last sentence.*)

I am honored and grateful to have the opportunity to write this "backward" forward. I'm even more honored that Kurt took a few ideas we had a number of years ago and turned them into something I could never have done on my own. I will always be thankful for that. You will be, too, from reading his book.

—**Lanny Donoho**

ABOUT THE AUTHOR

Kurt Kandler is the co-founder and Executive Director of The 410 Bridge—an organization committed to redefining the war on poverty.

Kurt and his wife of 32+ years—Erika—call Atlanta home and have an expanding family of four children and two grandchildren (for now . . .) He has an amazing duck tolling retriever named River who, like Kurt, finds her happy place on the water.

You can visit Kurt online at kurtkandler.com.

The 410 Bridge was founded in 2006. The organization is committed to redefining the war on poverty. Redefining what it means to win it, what it means for the people living in extreme poverty and, most importantly, redefining how we fight the battle together.

410 Bridge currently works in four countries and has served hundreds of thousands of people with clean water, economic development, education and health & wellness programs that are designed within a Christ-centered, community-initiated development model. To learn more about 410 Bridge, or support the work being done, please visit www.410Bridge.org.